NJ/W/£2.20

The Devil's Piper

The Devil's Piper

SUSAN PRICE

FABER AND FABER
3 Queen Square
London

First published in 1973
by Faber and Faber Limited
3 Queen Square, London WC1
Printed in Great Britain by
Unwin Brothers Limited, The Gresham Press
Old Woking, Surrey

ISBN 0 571 10420 7

Chapter 1

The two boys, one with a football under his arm, were walking along the canal tow-path, heading for the park. The park ran alongside the canal for some way; and there was a place where the park railings had been bent aside, and you could squeeze through, with some scratches from the privet hedge, into the park itself. It was much quicker to come by the canal and through the gap than to walk all the way round to the park's main gates.

The boys ducked under an overhanging bush, knowing that just in front of them was a place where the path had crumbled away in a semi-circle, leaving enough space for one person to hop across, and no more. Now two girls were crouched down in the narrow place, and from the look of it they had been washing their dolls' clothes in the water; because the little dresses were hooked over some fool's parsley to dry. The boys marched forward to claim their right of way.

It wasn't the done thing to be polite to girls, especially girls stupid enough to stop in such an awkward spot. So the bigger boy, the one with the ball, said, "Oi, you! Get out the road, we want to get past."

The nearer girl whipped round from her talk, showing a sharp, foxy face under yellow hair. "Who do you think you'm talkin' to?" she wanted to know, pushing her hair back behind her ears.

The boy tried to think of something that would shut her up before she got well started; and thought that he had found it. "I don't know," he said, "I've never seen anything like it afore. Now move, we want to get past."

"We don't want to move though," the yellow-haired girl said, hoity-toity. "We'm comfortable here, ain't we, Shirl?" The other girl nodded, with determination.

"Are yer goin' to move?" the boy asked threateningly. The two girls just sat there, daring him. "I'll thump yer," he said.

"An' yer'll get it back if yer do," the girl answered, cocking her chin at him.

"I'm bigger than you am," the boy growled, stretching himself up taller, but the yellow-haired girl came back with, "Don't matter, I'll kick an' scratch an' spit."

The boy had a sudden idea, pushed the football into his friend's hands, and snatched up half a dozen or so of the dolls' dresses. "You move," he said, "else we'll rip up these frocks an' throw 'em in the cut." He meant the canal.

The yellow-haired girl jumped up now and shouted, "You leave them be! You leave them be or else!"

"Or else what?" the bigger boy scoffed. "You wan 'em back, you move."

"You put the frocks back first," said the other girl, speaking for the first time. "Come on, Lin, sit down till

8

they put 'em back." But Lin wasn't sure what to do, and she still stood there, mouth open.

"You've got to move first," the boy said. He sorted quickly through the dolls' clothes and came up with an evening dress made of yellow satin. He tightened this between his hands. "I can rip it easy," he told the girls, "easy as anythin', if you don't move."

"Don't you dare!" Lin shouted. "I'll fetch a copper, I will! That's an offence, that is. They can put yer in prison for it!"

The boy just grinned at her and pulled at the little dress again so that it pleated into narrow creases and the stitches in the seams began to draw apart. Then an excited voice said, "Go on, go on, rip the thing!"

They all looked up in surprise and saw, a few feet away, sitting in the shade of a hawthorn tree, a man. It was a wonder that they hadn't seen him before, even though the colours of his clothes blended well with the green light from the leaves above him, making him seem shadowy around the edges. They stared at him for a minute or two, and then Lin said, "Shut up, you!"

She was bold enough to speak to him like that because she could see, even with him sitting down, that he wasn't very big. More the size of a boy than a man.

He slid down the bank from under the hawthorn tree, rolled on to his knees, then got up—and he certainly wasn't very big. Only a little taller than Lin herself. Very thick, black eyebrows he had, and a very wide mouth that seemed to stretch his face into a grin all the time. He wore a dark green jacket, with a strange shirt underneath that was white and baggy, and laced up the front instead of buttoning; and corduroy trousers, tied about the knees with string; and big, dirty, strongly-laced boots. On his head was a tall, lightish-green hat, with a black band, and a buckle on the band. But the funniest thing about him was that all his clothes were creased, with the creases full of dirt, as if he'd been buried. The first thought of the boy holding the football was that the man was a tramp, but he soon changed his mind. Not even a tramp can take off his hat and empty half a field out of it.

"Look at it," the little man said sadly. "And not even a funeral."

They couldn't understand this, and so ignored it, standing round and eyeing the strangely dressed man uneasily. The second boy, the quiet one, said suddenly, "You look like that drawin' in that book at school. The one showin' the navvies cuttin' the canal through. Don't he look just like that in them clothes?"

"True for you, true for you," the dirty man said. "They finished the old ditch so?" He glanced at the canal.

The two boys and the two girls looked at one another. Shirl began to pick up the rest of the dolls' clothes, while Lin took away those that the bigger boy held. He didn't try to stop her taking them.

The little man was taking no notice of them, but he had slipped from his pocket something that looked like a stick, and he was busy peeling dirt from it.

"What year is it now?" he asked, in an offhand sort of way. "1970 would it be, or thereabouts? Is the old place still the same?" He looked up and saw the blank faces in front of him. "Aah, come on now," he said. "How

10

many wars have they had? How many wonderful things have they made? How much damage have they done?"

None of them really knew what to say. Especially to the last question. But then the quiet boy, Chris, spoke up. "It's 1973," he said slowly. "There's been the first World War, and the second World War. . . ." His voice trailed away, and then he added, "There's the aeroplane, and the car. . . ." Again he stopped. He suddenly felt a right fool, answering questions that the man must know the answers to already.

But the man seemed satisfied. He nodded his head. "So they've got on to the World Wars, have they?" he asked. "Won't be long then, will it? Not now they have the flying machines." He stopped for a second, his face pulled into a grin as he wrestled with a stubborn bit of dirt, then asked, "What kind of flying things are they?"

Again it was difficult to know what to answer. Again Chris was the one to try. "All kinds," he said. "Jet planes. An' there's Concorde too."

"Is there now?" said the man, but he didn't seem to know what they were talking about. There was a question in his voice and face. Chris explained, "That's the one that can fly at twice the speed of sound."

The dirty little man's face lit up with delight. "That one! They have come on, have they not? That one already! But the quicker they build, the quicker they go." He seemed to think about that for a minute or two, as he rubbed at his stick, and then added, "And the quicker they go, the better."

11

The big boy took his football back from Chris and asked suspiciously, "If you know all about Concorde, why ask?"

The man lifted his stick up and looked along it. "We've always known your possibilities," he said. "Ever since you were whistled out of the mud. We just didn't know which ones you would make and which you wouldn't. But never mind—repent for the end is near!"

He must be mad, they all decided. He talked about nothing with a lot of words. Now he was looking at them again, leaning forward eagerly. He asked:

"Do people still believe in elves?"

A blank silence. Things went from bad to worse. "No," the boy with the football said, in a deep, disgusted voice. " 'Course they don't."

"They tell little kids about the fairies leavin' sixpence for their teeth, but that's only for little kids," Shirl said, after a pause.

"Do you believe in—elves an' fairies then?" Lin asked the man curiously.

The little man turned to look all about him, and smiled. He pushed his hat forward over his eyes with the palm of his hand, threw his head back, pushed his chest out, and said proudly, "Sure, it'd be hard for me not to. I am one."

They stared at him solemnly, not daring to laugh at him, and not wanting to miss anything by running away. The man, seeing their disbelief, slowly shrank to his right size.

"You'm an elf," said the boy with the football, flatly, with a mickey-taking nod of the head. The little man

12

nodded back. "The Irish kind," he said, trying to convince them. "A luchorpan."

"You mean leprechaun, don't you?" Lin asked, hoity-toity again.

"I do not! I mean luchorpan. I know what I am. And is it you that speaks the Irish?" Lin shut up. The dirty little man twisted a twig from a hawthorn bush above him, and began to poke holes with it into the stick he was cleaning. The stick looked more and more like a whistle. Shirl tried reasoning with him.

"If you was a fairy," she said, "you'd be able to fly and you ain't even got wings . . . all fairies are women anyroad."

The man stopped cleaning his flute and looked at her with an orange-brown eye from under a shaggy black brow. "Who's sayin' so?" he demanded. "Am I sayin' so that's standin' here an elf? Arrah, wouldn't I be a thing to make a donkey laugh with wings?"

"Well, you just can't be an elf then. Proves it, see!" Lin said bossily, hands on skinny hips.

"But if he is an elf, then he ought to know, didn't he?" Chris asked. He had an open mind.

"No such thing as elves, you're as daft as he is," Lin told him.

"No, listen," Chris urged. "They always say as ghosts don't exist, but it's never been *proved*, has it? Scientifically like, it's never been proved. There could be ghosts, so why not elves? It's never been *proved*. . . ."

"Come on, Chris, let's go," said the boy with the foot-ball, bored now.

13

"Oh, I don't want to go yet," Chris said mildly. "I'm just sayin', yer know, as it's never been proved. . . ."

"Yeah, we know, Einstein," Mike, the other boy, said. "Come on—or do you believe in fairies now?"

"Oh—just hang on a bit," Chris begged.

"Ah, come on!" Mike said. "I ain't got all day, have I?"

"I'll come with yer in a minute!" Chris snapped. "Just hang on a bit!"

"I don't want to, I . . ."

Then they all stopped quarrelling, stopped moving, stopped thinking, stopped breathing. They heard the sound of life—the sound grass makes when it grows, the sound of sun pouring like honey over a field.

They waited and they waited, terrified that the sound had ended and would never come again.

But it came, like Spring. The circles made by a stone as it falls into the green of a canal, the gleam of a fish belly, the long rippling of grass in a wind, the waves of the sea, a wild rose bud softly bursting—a green and yellow tune, a tune that tasted of the chewed white stems of young grass.

The tune finished on a long whistle—the whistle of a man, maybe, when he calls a dog on the hillside. It left the four townies staring breathlessly at grass and hawthorn that was greener than it had been a few minutes before; and the noise from the road above the canal had faded to silence. Far overhead a skylark sang in the peacefulness.

Everything returned to normal, with the crash of the lorries and the dust they threw up, the dirty paper that

14

they whirled to the side of the road. The skylark's song was lost in the din. Mike, with the football, Chris, Shirl and Lin all looked to the luchorpan and caught him in the act of lowering the penny-whistle from his mouth.

"Did you play that?" Mike asked, in a voice that had become throaty and hard to speak with.

"I did, what do yer use for eyes? Me old blower still works, the darlin'. I thought the wet might have got at her."

"If you played *that*," Chris said, through the thick stuff that was gluing his words in, "I'll believe you're a lep-luchorpan."

The luchorpan looked round at the others with a smile—a smile that was crafty and a bit like a dog's when he hangs his mouth open. "The Old One!" he said. "I never thought that the English had sense at all. Now, my name's Toole O'Dyna." One after the other, they told him their names, and he tried to look surprised at the sound of them. Then he grinned and said, "Now we all know each other, and I'm glad of that! I hate to beg from strangers. Is there e'er a chance of a meal?"

He got no answer, only a doubtful silence. So he seemed to forget all about food, saying instead, "We'd better be gettin' to the town, had we not? Wait a minute though." He sat down on the tow-path, took off his big boots, knotted the laces and slung them around his neck. "Boots are for workin' in, not walkin' in," he explained.

He stood up again, pushed his shoulders back, tilted his hat to an adventurous angle, and set off down the tow-

15

path towards the lock-gates, the path to the road, and the town, with the four others tailing after him, even Mike.

"Please, Mr. Toole, will yer play us another tune?" Lin asked.

Chapter 2

The luchorpan was surprised when his first car, and then an overloaded, speeding lorry, passed them on the road. He jumped sharply, shouted in fright, choked and coughed in the dust thrown up by the wheels. But he had braced himself for anything, and by the time they had reached the first bend he had worked out that cars were only machines driven by men, and that if you kept out of their way, they would keep out of yours, like bees.

The buildings in the town, too, were a shock. They were all so big, all built out of brick, all with glass in large windows. And many of the windows were filled with bright, strange things: things that not even the most powerful imagination could have thought up by itself. But the shops and houses didn't move at high speeds, and so, apart from walking at a good distance from the walls, the luchorpan didn't let them bother him. After all, a luchorpan spends his whole life going from one time to another, and he'd be in nothing but trouble if he let every new thing frighten him.

Now he came back to the question of food—in a crafty, roundabout way. "To whose house are we goin' then?" he asked carelessly.

17

The other four were quiet, not wanting to answer. Then Mike told him straight out, without trying to be polite, "You can't come to mine, me mother wouldn't like it."

"That's right," Lin said. "She's as mean as you are—wouldn't give nobody a cold."

"You can talk," Mike answered back.

"You can come to our house," Shirl offered. "Me Mom'll be out till come six."

Lin didn't like being put in the shade. "He can come to mine if he likes!" she squealed.

And Chris, who didn't like arguing, and who didn't like visitors coming to his home, felt that something inside him made him say, "He don't want to go to *your* house, he can come to mine."

"Go to yours!" Lin screamed. "What's he want to go to your house for? You an' your stuck-up lot! He can come to our house an' have a cup o' tea an'—an' some bread an' jam!"

Mike said, "I think you'm all daft—fancy askin' him to come an' eat yer out of house an' home. An' him an escaped loony an' all!"

"He's a luchorpan!" Shirl hissed.

"Saftness!" Mike said. He was beginning to forget all about the tune the little man had played.

"You shut up, you!" Lin cried. "Nobody asked you for your four-penn'orth!"

During the quarrel they had been walking through the streets of the town, getting lost among the shoppers, leaning around large women and larger bags to shout at each other. The luchorpan followed close behind

18

them, so as not to get lost, listening to their fighting with what seemed to be a pleased half-smile. At last he said regretfully, "Whose house is nearest? Tell me that."

"Ours is just round the corner," Shirl chirped up quickly.

"Right you are then," said the luchorpan. "We'll go there, so. It'll save us a lot of time."

He was led around a corner, away from the main shopping street into a smaller one, lined with butchers', grocers', small dress and hat shops. The luchorpan was interested in them all, especially in the butchers'. He sighed deeply at the sight of half a pig hanging from a hook.

In the next street there were small factories, offices, scrapyards, houses and the museum. It was an unusual street to find a museum in, but it was an unusual museum. It had been a row of old labourers' cottages, reminder of the time when the town had been farm-land, but now all the inside walls were knocked down, and the museum exhibits had been arranged enticingly within. The luchorpan recognised the cottages, and he was fascinated by them.

"I can remember," he said, "when all these cottages was lived in, an' kept as neat as ninepence, all except the one on the end—aah, she was a baggage."

He hung around the old cottages, peering in through the tiny windows, and trying to see what was in them now. "There was an old lady an' her husband in this one," he told them. "Kept pigs, they did, an' reminded Tobin—Tobin McGraw, that is—reminded him of his Da'. She gave me an' Tobin a drink of water once."

19

His new friends were impatient. They couldn't care less about the cottages, or the museum inside. "Come on, Mr. Toole," Shirl said. "You want something to eat, don't you?"

"And you said you'd play us another tune," Lin put in.

But Toole O'Dyna was not to be hurried. He moved aside for an elderly lady who came out of the museum, took off his hat for her, and then turned back.

"In this one there was a man couldn't keep away from the drink, and he hadn't a head that could take it either. Paralysed he used to be, and his Missis would lock him out. Every night of his life! We used to bring him up to the bothies with us, and he'd sleep it off. He reminded Tobin of his Da's pigs as well, he snored so loud. Only we lost him one night."

That phrase caught Mike's attention. He couldn't quite see the meaning of it. "You lost him?" he asked in puzzlement.

"We did. We was carryin' him up to the bothies, me an' Tobin an' another feller, an' we lost him. We put him down somewhere, and when we come for him, he was lost, an' we didn't see him after that."

"But what had happened to him?" Mike persisted. "Where had he gone?"

"Do I know?" cried the luchorpan, getting angry. "I do not! We put him down an' when we came back there he was—gone! How do I know where he was?"

"But the next day! Didn't you go and find out what had happened to him?" Mike argued.

"Listen to me." The luchorpan was very patient.

20

"Three times I have told you. He was *lost*. How could I ask him when he was lost?"

Light dawned on them. "You mean he was never found?" Mike asked quietly.

"I didn't look," answered the luchorpan over his shoulder, as he went on to the next cottage. "Why should I care? It was his time. He probably fell into the river. It was just near there."

"Poor man," Shirl said, but the luchorpan was cheerful. "Arrah! He was no better than any of the rest of you."

Chris had been listening very thoughtfully. Now, as the luchorpan squinted through another window, he asked, "Mr. Toole? Did all those people *really* live here?"

"Didn't I just say so?"

"When did they live, then?" Chris asked.

"Oh Old One! When I was here last, when else? Sure, I'm thinkin' you dull! When we was diggin' the canals. 1773 it would be, and the man who lived there was named Russel." He pointed to the last cottage but one and watched Chris carefully.

"My name's Russel," Chris said.

"Fancy that now, isn't it a small world?" the luchorpan asked, apparently surprised. "I'll tell yer about him one of these days. Are we ne'er going to this house at all? I haven't had a bite for two hundred years. I could eat a cow entirely."

Shirl sighed, and Lin told him, "We've been askin' yer to come for the last half-hour!"

"What a lie!" said the luchorpan indignantly. "Would I stand here that great length of time when I'm clammin'

21

to death on me feet? Would I hang about here with me belly thinkin' me throat's cut?"

"Oh, come on then," Shirl said.

Shirl's house wasn't very far away from the museum. It was one of a row of big, old houses, now divided into two for two families each. They were grubby, and looked sorry for themselves, with their tiny, over-grown gardens, and the grass and stink-weed sprouting from their corners.

Shirl opened the back door with a big key that hung around her neck on a piece of string, and let the others into the kitchen. But the luchorpan hung back. With one hand on the wooden frame of the door he leaned inside and sniffed. He looked suspiciously at the lino-covered floor, at the walls covered with bright paper, at the stove, the sink, the crowded dresser, the hall which led away into more closed boxes of rooms—and at the one window that he could see, the little one, high in the kitchen wall, half-covered by plastic curtains. He backed away from the door towards the garden fence.

"Well, come in," Shirl said, standing by the door.

"No—no, I don't think I will." The luchorpan was unsure of himself for the first time. He had tight hold, with both hands, of the chestnut-paling fence between Shirl's house and the next one.

"You've got to come in if you want something to eat," Shirl told him.

From where he was, by the fence, the luchorpan peered in through the door. But it was no use. "No, no, I won't. I—I don't like them big places," he explained. "The bothies is all right, but I don't like them big places.

I'll tell yer what. You pass the eatin' stuff to me here, an' I'll eat it here."

"All right," Shirl said uncertainly. "All right. If you'm sure you don't want to come in."

But as she went into the living-room to fetch the teapot from the table, she had an idea. "We can have a picnic like," she said, coming back into the kitchen. "Eat it in the yard. You can go an' sit in the yard, an' me an' Lin'll get it ready."

So the boys went out and led the luchorpan round to the back yard, where there was a square of dusty concrete, two naked, ugly, grey chestnut-paling fences, and a long strip of garden, ending in a brick wall, which grew mostly grass.

Inside the house Shirl made jam sandwiches, while Linda made the tea. They took the meal out to the yard.

They found the boys sitting on the concrete, watching the luchorpan, who was walking round and round in circles on the strip of garden. The tray they put down beside the boys, along with sandwiches and tea-pot. The sandwiches started to disappear as Chris and Mike grabbed them. It was some minutes before a voice said, "Could yer not bring that bread over here?"

Shirl looked up and saw the luchorpan standing at the very edge of the garden, but not coming on to the concrete. She took the plate over to him, and he lifted sandwiches with both hands. He explained his reason for not leaving the garden. "I don't like that hard stuff, I don't like it an' I'm not goin' near it more than I need to." He opened his mouth as wide as the Mersey Tunnel, stuffed in three sandwiches at once, chewed hard, his eyes

23

closing, and added thickly "That hard stuff—it doesn't grow an' it doesn't let anythin' grow. It's no good at all."

"Oh," Shirl said. "Shall I bring you some tea?"

The luchorpan frowned at her. When he had swallowed, with an ostrich-like gulp, he asked. "Tee? What's that at all?"

"*Tea*," Shirl said. "*Tea*. You know, you drink it."

"Tee? Drink it?" The luchorpan scowled in bafflement, and took another huge bite.

"Tea!" Shirl cried. "You make it with hot water. You know, with tea-leaves. And you drink it with milk and sugar."

The luchorpan's eyebrows jumped up as he realised what she was talking about. "Tay!" he cried. "Yer mean tay! Oh aye, yer can bring me some of that, I ne'er had any before. I only heard tell of it. Hey, wait a minute, bring that bread back here! I like the sweet stuff it has in it."

So Shirl gave him more sandwiches before taking the plate back to the others, and later, when it was poured, she took him the biggest, hottest and strongest cup of tea. He sipped it cautiously at first, but he must have liked it, because he drained the tea-leaves against his teeth, and asked for another cup, and another after that. With each cup he wanted more sugar. And after the third cup he said that if there was any bread left he would eat it for them to save waste. Shirl passed him the last sandwiches, thinking that perhaps two hundred years without food did make you grabbing.

"You *will* play another tune, won't you, Mr. Toole,"

24

Chris asked, as the luchorpan was starting on these last sandwiches, standing up with the plate in one hand.

"You promised you would," Lin said.

Still chewing, the luchorpan answered, "I didn't either. An' supposin' that I did, what's it matter? What's a promise worth anyway?"

"We were taught," Lin said primly, "that promises should be kept."

"You were taught wrong so," the luchorpan said flatly. "If a man wants to do a thing he doesn't have to promise. Promises is only made when a man doesn't want to do a thing."

They all agreed with him really, though they'd never heard anyone come right out and say it like that. Especially someone older than themselves. As for the luchorpan, he had no particular views on promises—they weren't in his line. But a luchorpan will argue with his own finger-ends if there's no one else about, and he will change his opinions when he looks like being beaten.

"Anyway," said the luchorpan now, since he'd won without trying, "I have to be very careful with me tunes."

"Why?" Chris asked.

"Why?" The luchorpan seemed to be astounded by this stupid question. "Why? Because they're dangerous, that's for why! What way else? I can play Spring and Summer, Life and Death, Autumn and Winter, Anger, Love, Hate, Light, Dark, Loneliness, Sadness, Happiness, Sleep, Forgetting, Hunger, Rain, Sun, Blue, Yellow, Green, Black, Sweet and Sour. I can't be playin' those classes of tunes just any time, can I now?"

The others sat, not for the first time that day, in dead

25

silence, staring. They didn't know what to make of it. They'd never heard anyone claim anything like it.

"Can you *really* play those things?" Chris asked, on an outlet breath.

"Can you *really* this, can you *really* that . . .?" muttered the luchorpan.

Mike spoke up. "Course he can't. I've never heard such a pack of saftness in me life. I think he's escaped from the loony bin, and us here sittin' with him." He leant forward and spat out a mouthful of tea. "What have yer put in this tea? It's horrible! The milk's sour."

Shirl took the cup from him and smelt it. "It is too," she said. She sniffed at the bottle. "An' this is. That's funny. It wasn't when we brought it out, was it, Lin?"

"What's a loony-bin?" asked the luchorpan; and when it was explained to him, added, "I was right so."

"But *can* you really play all those things?" Chris asked again.

"Can I? Can I?" the luchorpan mimicked. "Would I say so if I couldn't?"

"What shall I do," Shirl asked everyone, "with this milk sour?"

"It's nothin' to worry about," the luchorpan assured her. "I've had all I want, though it wasn't much to be sure. Bread only fills yer for a little while. I'll be going now, thankin' yer very much for the food and drink. I needed it. If yer look around in corners after I've gone maybe yer'll find somethin' that . . .'"

"But you haven't played us a tune!" Lin wailed.

"You promised," Chris said, and Shirl stared up at the elf as he stood above them, his hat cocked to one side.

26

Even Mike was anxious. The luchorpan grinned. It was a slow, wide, wicked grin that lit up little orange flames behind the brown of his eyes.

"Is it a tune yer wantin'?" he asked, soft. "Come with me then, I'll be playin' later, sure." There seemed to be faint music in his words.

They all scrambled to their feet in a great hurry. "I'll make more sandwiches," Shirl said.

"Yer won't, yer won't," the luchorpan said. "Yer don't need to carry food when yer travel with a luchorpan. I'm goin' now anyway, an' yer'll lose me if yer stop."

That left no time to clear up, or to make more sandwiches, or anything else. They ran after the elf to the gate, and followed him back down the road, towards the canal that he had helped to dig two hundred years before. The luchorpan, they noticed, stepped along the pavement as if the concrete and tarmac were red-hot and burning his feet. Whenever he could he stepped on to a grass verge.

"Do yer have that sayin' still?" he asked. "That work goes before pleasure? I never did believe in it. I'm all for takin' me pleasure first, if I can be arrangin' it that way." He glanced at Mike. "I got some work to do, but I'm goin' to see how the old place has changed first before I get on with that. That's what I enjoy most, seein' how things have changed. Aah, that time after the Black Death, it was wonderful! Hardly any people left at all, just the land. Sure, I thought we were goin' to be rid of you! But you're too blessed clever, that's what you are. Too blessed clever, by half."

When Shirl's mother came home, with the baby asleep

27

in his push-chair, she was very annoyed to find the tray outside in the yard, with a bottle of milk, a crumby plate, a sugar bowl, five cups and two or three spoons. She didn't mind Shirl taking the things into the yard; she didn't mind Shirl leaving her the washing-up; but she did think that the girl might have brought the things into the house again.

She was even more angry to find the milk was sour— and no wonder, leaving it in the sun for God knows how long! She'd have a few words to say to that young lady when she came home. Shirl was off playing now, probably, with never a thought for her mother who had to do all the work.

She went into the house, her mouth tight, and her eyes angry, put the baby to sleep on the settee, cleared the table off, and started the washing-up, saying, "Hello," absently to Jon, Shirl's older brother, when he came in from the football match.

A few minutes later he was back in the kitchen, asking, "What's for tea then?" and when she didn't answer, "What's to eat then? Hey, Muth! What're yer makin' for tea?"

Mrs. Plummer hissed tiredly between her teeth as she reached for the towel. "Oh, I don't know. Go an' sit down, will yer? I'm tired."

"So'm I, Muth," Jon said, reaching for a glass from the cupboard. "An' I've had nothin' to eat all day. Hurry up with the tea."

"Give me a chance!" Mrs. Plummer shouted. "I've just come in from shoppin' an' Shirley ain't done the washin'-up. Can't yer wait for a minute? Hey, an' that's yer Father's beer, you can tell him why there ain't none left, I'm not goin' to."

"Oh for God's sake!" Jon said. "I'm only havin' a drop. Take the dust off me throat. Honestly, this house! Yer'd think I was askin' for the moon 'cos I want me tea." He was crouching just inside the pantry, pouring beer from the can into his glass.

Mrs. Plummer calmed down a little. "All right then," she said. "Have a look around in there somewhere. I think there's a tin of stewing steak. Yer can have that with chips. An' an egg. That suit yer?"

"Oh yeah! Great!" Jon took a swig from his glass, and sorted through the tins, bottles and packets on the pantry shelf. He found the tin of stewing-steak and took it out to his mother. She was drying a saucepan.

"Open it an' tip the meat in here," she said, passing him the pan.

As he was scooping the meat out with a knife he'd found, and thinking how like Kit-E-Kat it was, he asked, "Muth, can I have batter on me chips? It's more fillin' that way."

"Y-e-s, I suppose so," Mrs. Plummer said, without enthusiasm. "You'll have to go an' fetch another bottle of milk though, this is sour. Shirl left it in the yard all afternoon."

He went quickly down the hall, before she could start on about his sister, and fetched another bottle of milk back to the hot, greasy kitchen. But when he opened it, that milk was sour too. And the next bottle. In fact, all the milk in the house was sour. Mrs. Plummer couldn't understand it. She sniffed first at one bottle, then at the other, then sniffed at them both again.

29

"Well," she said. "Well. That *is* funny. They warn't standin' in the sun, was they, Jon? They *was* down on the floor in the shade? I don't get it then. I just can't understand it. Well, yer can't have batter on yer chips, that's for sure. Go an' tip this down the drain, there's a good lad. I'll get yer tea on now."

Jon grumbled at having no batter as he poured the milk away, but at least his tea was on the way now. His mother was peeling potatoes, and the stewing steak was warming beside a kettle for tea. He emptied the tea-pot and put the tea into it—five spoons.

"I wonder where our Shirl is?" said his mother. "Oh, we've gotta have some milk for the tea—will yer nip round to Vera next door an' get some?"

"Yeah," Jon said, "in a minute." He went back into the living-room and sat down in an arm-chair, with his legs up over the arm, and a 'Beano' to read. When his mother cracked his egg in the kitchen, the smell took him by the throat and shook him, even from the next room. Gagging, and fanning the air with his comic, Jon stumbled back to the kitchen. The air was almost green with the evil stench.

"Bad egg," his mother gasped as she wrenched open the door and leaned out to breathe.

"Bad egg!" he said, and it was certainly the worst bad egg that he had ever come into contact with, worse even than the chemical 'bad eggs' that they put in stink-bombs.

Just then Mr. Plummer came in. He got two full lungs of the kitchen air, and doubled up with a sob.

"Bad egg," his son told him, without sympathy.

"An' all the milk's sour," said his wife. "I just don't understand it."

"Bad management," said Mr. Plummer, shortly.

"Oh, that ain't right." Mrs. Plummer looked as if she might cry at the drop of a bad egg. "This is the first time anythin' like it has happened, an' well you know it! Oh, I don't feel like cookin' though, an' that's a fact."

"All right," Mr. Plummer said calmly. "Send Jon for some fish an' chips." He lifted his voice to reach his son in the living-room. "Oi you! Hairy! You don't lay off my beer, I'll do for you!"

"Hey, Muth!" Jon yelled back. "The bread's mouldy, an' the cheese, an' the butter's rancid!"

Chapter 3

Miss Virginia Jenns walked along the street behind two
miniature Yorkshire terriers, with blue collars and leads.
They were washed and brushed, and both had the hair
tied back from their eyes with pink bows. The lady herself carried, in one gloved hand, a small camera, complete
with flash-bulb.

It had been a birthday present from her niece, who
lived with her. A perfect birthday present, Miss Jenns
thought, for she was devoted to photographs. Until now
she had had to take all her pictures with a very old, stiff
box-camera; and always she had had to take them out of
doors, but now, with this brand new small camera, with
flash-bulbs . . . .

So Miss Jenns, this Saturday morning, was snap-happy.
She had already taken two pictures of her niece, one with
the Yorkshire terriers and one without; and two pictures of
the Yorkshire terriers, one indoors and one out of doors;
she had taken a picture of the next-door-neighbour, and
one of the next-door-neighbour's cat; and also one of the
next-door-neighbour's splendid forsythia bush. And she
had brought the camera with her on the dogs' walk in
case something else photograph-worthy caught her eye.

32

She reached the corner on which the museum stood, and was about to turn it, glad to get away from these dreadful factories and scrap-yards at last, when she saw the man.

He was standing outside the museum, apparently arguing with some children. There was nothing unusual in that, the children from these streets so very cheeky—it was the man she stared at. Dressed in such strange clothes. She was about to dismiss him as one of those rather frightening young men who were so common in the High Street on Saturdays, when she remembered about some places of historical interest which were employing people to dress up in clothes of the period, and loaf around providing historical colour for the eyes of the visitors.

Almost before she had thought about it, Miss Jenns had lifted her camera and taken a picture of the man. Then she was ashamed of her rudeness. Well, she told herself, he *was* unusual, and Rosalyn, her niece, was very interested in history.

That evening, after tea, she had to confess that she had used up all twenty of the frames on the film.

"That doesn't matter. I bought it for you to do that," Rosalyn said, without looking round from the television. "I'll take them round to Mr. Hadley for you later, if you've really used all twenty. When this is over."

When the music for the end of the programme started, and the names were falling down the screen, Rosalyn took her aunt's camera to Mr. Hadley, who lived only a few doors away. He was a keen photographer himself, and when he found out that his neighbour took photographs, he offered to develop them for her.

Rosalyn left the film with him and came back later, to see if he had finished the photographs. He had and ran upstairs to fetch them. They weren't quite dry, he said, but near enough.

"There's one unusual one," he said with a smile, a cigarette jerking between his lips, as he flapped quickly through photographs of dogs, cats, children, flowers and interestingly shaped trees; and finally he picked out one and gave it to her to look at.

It was a picture of the museum, but what made it unusual was the group of figures in the foreground. There were four children and she recognised them as four who attended the school where she taught. They were all facing towards some central object, but in the picture this object was missing. There was a whitish patch, an emptiness, a space. A solid space, because part of two of the children was missing also—hidden behind the gap. One, a boy named, she believed, Mike, could only be seen from the shoulder up, the rest of him was lost. The other was a girl, a fair-haired girl, and she had half a leg blotted out. It was as if the space had been cut out, or painted over. When you looked closely, you saw that the patch was roughly man-shaped.

"Very unusual," said Mr. Hadley, his cigarette wagging furiously. "Very unusual. I've never seen anything like it. How did your aunt get that effect?"

"I don't know," Rosalyn said, staring at the picture in her hand. "I don't think she tried any tricks like that. It looks just as if someone were standing there, but hasn't been developed with the rest of the picture. It *is* very odd, isn't it? How much do I owe you, Mr. Hadley?"

"Nothing! Nothing at all. It's no trouble to me to do those little pictures for you."

Miss Jenns was eager to see her photographs, exclaiming over how well the tulips had come out, and how *sweet* her little dogs looked. It was some time before Rosalyn could get her to look at the photograph with the white patch. When she did look, she said:

"Oh, that's the one I took of the man outside the museum! Rude of me, I thought, without asking his permission, but I know how interested you are in history. It hasn't come out very well, has it?"

"Mr. Hadley said he'd never seen anything like it. Was the man where the patch is in the picture?"

Miss Jenns turned the photograph about, studying it. "I *imagine* he was," she said. "He's not anywhere else."

Rosalyn laughed. "He must be a ghost, Aunt Gin, and so he doesn't show up on film! The museum's haunted. It'll have twice as many visitors now."

"Or he might be a leprechaun," said Miss Jenns, with a silly little smile.

Rosalyn smiled too, amused. Miss Jenns had once shyly shown her niece some poetry that she had written when younger. It had been all about tiny little fairies making swing-boats from hazel-nut shells, and 'jumping on their fairy steeds and vanishing in the night'. Miss Jenns had not changed much in growing older.

"Of course, he's a little large to be a leprechaun," she said.

"Leprechauns always were bigger than other fairies,"

35

Rosalyn said seriously, as if she had made a life-long study of fairies. "May I borrow it, Aunt Gin? The picture, I mean? I'd like to show it around at school."

"Of course you can, dear, if you want to. Don't lose it, though, whatever you do. It's the only picture I have of a real leprechaun."

Rosalyn couldn't tell if she was joking or not.

Chapter 4

The luchorpan set off across the stale concrete of the pavements, straight for the canal, the earth tow-paths and the grass. But there were always other things, new and fascinating things, despite the paving and tarmac, that led him off, away from the waterway.

Streets of large houses, their brickwork smoothed over with white plaster; bay windows with lacy curtains, fresh paint, neat, glossy porches, and lovely, if small, gardens. The luchorpan wandered down these streets, staggering on the concrete, stumbling up and down the gutter, mouth agape. He seemed dumb-struck. At last he whispered to Chris, "Who is it that lives here?"

"What do yer mean?" Chris asked.

"They must be terrible grand people," the luchorpan murmured, staring up at a house with gleaming green and white shutters.

"Grand people?" Chris said. "No. They're just ordinary —well, better off than us—David Smith comes from round here, don't he, Mike? He goes to Grammar School."

"We'll go to the Comp," Mike added, "thank God."

The luchorpan never even heard them. "Ordinary

people!" he said. "It's—it's—I'm banjaxed! Sure, the house of Shirl was like I'd never seen before—but these! Will yer look at all the glass! And not a puddle in it! And the doors! Old One, yer frighten me sometimes, yer do that!"

He stepped on, and gave himself a brave swagger, shoulders swinging, feet out to the side. He tilted his hat to a more reckless angle, trying to feel the equal of any in these grand houses. And they were grand. He'd thought Shirl's house wonderful enough, but these— they were grand.

The two boys and the girls, coming behind, watching him walking so cockily. They also watched him come to a letter-box, and step off the pavement, in order to prowl around it in a complete circle, stiff as a fighting cock. From a distance away he bent at the knees to peer in at the black slot.

"It's for letters," Chris said. "You write a letter, and put it in the box through that hole, and then the postman comes and takes it where you want it to go."

"Ah—that," said the luchorpan. "They would have that in grand streets like this."

At the end of the street was a house which, because it was on a corner, had a garden twice the size of any other. The garden had a great many flowers: daffodils, tulips, an early rose or two; gay, bushy borders, ornamental, feathery grass, and small bushes. There was one tree, tall, dark green, with spindly branches like insects' legs. Both the branches of the tree, and the thin trunk were covered in spines. They leaned on the iron scroll-work gate, and looked at it.

"And what class of tree is *that*?" asked the luchorpan dazedly.

"It's a monkey-puzzle tree," Mike said.

"Because it would puzzle a monkey to climb it. It being all over spikes," Chris explained.

The luchorpan gawped up at its tall top, and looked it over all the way down. "The man that's growin' it's a liar," he said definitely. "I've never seen a thing like it. Not even when the whisky was bad."

"There's a lot of them," Chris said, "in gardens like these."

But the luchorpan had made up his mind. "It's not a good thing," he said. "It's not natural, it's not natural at all. Like this concrete stuff. It makes me feet itch. Let's be away to the cut."

He seemed to know where the canal was, for he took the quickest way, even walking through gardens. "All these flowers!" he said. "Flowers! Where are the 'taties and the peas?"

Nor did he approve of the canal when they reached it. He saw oil glinting dully with its seven colours, making the water greasy. A pram rested on so much rubbish that its wheels, with their rusty spokes, were above water. Cans floated along, slowly spinning. Toffee papers, cartons, packets, bottles and cellophane wrappings were thicker in the grass than cuckoo-spit. The further they walked along the tow-path, the thicker became the litter, and the dust, and the dead fish. The luchorpan began to mutter to himself. He started throwing his arms about as if he were making a speech.

"Look at it," he begged no one in particular. "Look at

39

it! All the filth and the dirt! Do the human kind get any better? They do not! They get worser and worser. They are burying the old place beneath their leavin's! Wouldn't it be better if they buried themselves?"

He got very miserable, he talked himself into it, Shirl thought. He decided that he no longer had the strength to carry his boots and shied them into the canal, remarking bitterly, "Everythin' else is in there!" He was in for a bigger disappointment, Shirl told herself, when they reached the common.

The canal, at one point, snipped a corner off the common, and here they climbed up from the tow-path. The common was a miserable, windy place, marshy in hollows, grown over with long, dull, green-brown grass. It was only 'the common' because it was no good for anything else. There were colliery roads all underneath it, so that the ground was always shifting and sinking, and couldn't even be built on. Everywhere it was scarred with car-tracks and pot-holes, with water lying muddy in the grooves. There were paper and plastic cups, and ice-cream tubs scattered over the whole area, but piled most thickly around the iron wastepaper baskets, which were disguised as piles of logs. Old yellow newspapers blew about like winged things, and plastered themselves around the thin, scrubby trees. And in the distance marched the stiff ranks of the forestry commission.

The luchorpan stared about as they stumbled over the tussocky grass. He took off his hat and held it to his chest dramatically, as if he were attending a funeral. He said nothing.

They came to where the uneven ground dipped down in a bowl, the sides furred with long yellow grass. At the bottom lay greasy water, smeared with oil from a rusty tin can tipped over nearby, and cold, grey mud. Cans, bottles, flasks, even an old tyre, were embedded in the grey slime. The luchorpan dropped down as if his legs had been kicked from under him. He lifted his whistle, and the four others crouched beside him, eyes shining, ready to lap up the music.

The tune rose in a high shrill stream. It seemed to come from a long, lonely distance away, like the curlew's call. The notes were smoke—blue wood smoke that drifted . . . drifted . . . and disappeared. It told of friends— friends like Tobin McGraw, perhaps, who, a long, almost forgotten time ago, had laughed with you over a joke and had then vanished. The flowing hair of a woman who never was, and of a woman who had laughed, smiled, warmly lived, but was dead and ice now; of a tree that grew, that was strong, that became weak and old, choked with ivy, that cracked and fell; and of the ghoulish toadstools that fed on its corpse; a song of all these things, and of the smoke, and the lonely curlew, the smell of cooking meat, the smell of dirt after rain, and mouldering leaves, all the fading things, and the covering of them by the floating smoke, their withering beyond recall.

Shirl felt the tears behind her eyes, and blinked with her eyebrows held high. She was ashamed to cry, but the force of tears crowded in her throat, trying to break out, and her face collapsed, her mouth spreading over most of it. Tears poured down her cheeks. Beside her Lin was squealing like a stuck pig, and Chris was snuffling. Mike was still fighting it.

But music the like of that! It wasn't to be found anywhere else on earth. They would stay close by the luchorpan.

Chapter 5

They had walked a long way. They had trekked up and down the neat lines of trees in the forestry commission; had trudged the length and dreary breadth of the common, stopping by a black, muddy, oily pond, with a plastic detergent bottle floating in it.

They had followed the ridgeway along the top of the old hills, above all the towns and the factories. These hills had been spared because they were useless, like the common; only a rough field had climbed up them, here and there, with its hen-runs and brick walls. From the ridge they could look down on a tarmacked, busy road known as 'The Portway'. It had been an ancient track when the Saxons had first come to this part of the country—and all the oldest names in this district were Saxon. From the time that men had begun trading salt had been carried along the Portway track, on their backs, which was why it was still called the Portway. Now the only salt carried along it, if any, went on the backs of lorries. Chris thought it a good thing. Easier than carrying it.

From the ridge they could see rows and rows of prison-like flats, built out of grey cement cubes; whole streets of blackened factories with tiny windows; and patches of half-dead grass that made the onlooker's stomach sink with hopelessness. The luchorpan sighed and turned away, head down, hand twitching his hat over his already lowered eyes. And then they came to a place where even the hills had been scooped away, leaving the dirt underneath coal-black and crumbling. Rubbish had been thrown into the cut-away hollow. Oil-drums, a torn-out gas-stove, a rotting mattress with damp straw spilling out, and bed-spring ribs poking through the cover; a car, tyre-less, door-less, bonnet-less, seat-less, with all its windows smashed and many parts of its engine missing. As the luchorpan looked down in horror at what had been done to the hill, Mike told him, "They took the dirt from here in dirty great lorries all the way down to the main road, to fill a marl-hole up with it. They're buildin' a power station on it now, on where the marl-hole was, yer know."

The luchorpan turned away, saying nothing, and led them back along the ridgeway, his eyes on the ground. He was thinking deeply about something.

"I'm hungry," Lin said to Shirl. None of them had anything to eat with them, and it was no use talking to the elf. He didn't hear them. They couldn't go home either. If they left they might never find Toole O'Dyna again. Nor his penny-whistle.

The luchorpan led them, without seeming to notice anything, carefully around all houses, going by the rough fields and waste-ground that surrounded the little town. It was a long, tiring way to follow, and one that didn't seem to go anywhere. Tired, sweaty, dusty, very

44

hungry, they asked the luchorpan where he was heading for. He never even glanced at them. Shirl tugged at his sleeve to repeat the question, and got such an evil look from under the shade of the green hat that she almost fell over. Her fingers suddenly felt as if she were holding them in a fire, and she snatched them from the cloth of the luchorpan's coat, and put their reddened ends into her mouth. The elf walked on, ignoring her squeak. They all trailed after him. He never thought for a moment that they wouldn't. They were his company.

By full dark they were again crossing the common. It was much harder in the dark, and they stumbled and fell over the rough ground. Chris splashed in a puddle in one of his falls, and then the wind felt much colder than before. His fingers were growing very numb.

The luchorpan never tripped, never seemed so much as unsteady. Night was his time. Day was an inconvenience that he could stand for the purpose of business. Night was cooler, soothing to the eyes and mind, it was damper, it was closer and safer, it was more relaxed. It was the easy time.

He led his complaining troop to a shallow hollow, edged with thin trees. It was in rising ground, this hollow, so it was dry, and the trees and the banks gave a little shelter from the wind. The luchorpan began to go from tree to tree, picking up the branches that lay at the foot of each trunk, to make a fire.

"I'm that hungry," Lin said, "I can feel all me belly empty. An' it keeps makin' funny noises."

"An' ours do," Mike said. "But we don't moan."

"You do! You said. . . ."

45

"Not like you say it I didn't!" Mike shouted.

The luchorpan came back and dropped the branches he had collected in a rattling heap. He squatted down beside them. Chris watched him idly to take his mind off his rumbling belly. He expected to see the elf take matches or a lighter from a pocket, but the luchorpan just shuffled the wood about a little, and then laid his left hand on top of the pile, palm up, fingers and thumb all touching in a point. He waited.

Chris watched, his interest caught, while the others argued and chatted about how hungry they were. He saw the tips of the luchorpan's fingers glow dully red, he saw the elf screw his eyes shut and clench his teeth. The air in the hollow grew hot and tight, yellowish. Chris felt his head throb like a drum, as it did sometimes before a thunderstorm—and then there was a spark, a flicker of light, and the luchorpan held, between his finger-tips, a bright yellow flame, that leaned over in the wind and blew ragged at the end.

The luchorpan opened his eyes, saw the little fire spear, and grinned. He carefully held it to twig after twig, until they caught and crackled, and allowed the flame to run along them to the bigger branches. Then he opened the fingers of his hand and the flames fell, like a leaf or a golden coin, into the pile of wood, and disappeared. Chris blinked, released from his fascination, wondering if he had really seen the luchorpan holding a flame in his hand. But he could feel the heat of the fire now, and it made the rest of him very cold. He crawled nearer to it and gave up useless wonderings.

The others came too, thankful for the warmth, but it

didn't make them forget their hunger. Lin began again to tell how empty her stomach was, and how long it had been since she had eaten. She had told them all this five times already.

"Wait here," the luchorpan said at last, and walked away through the thin railings of the trees.

"Do yer think he'll come back?" Chris asked.

"He'd better," Lin said, as if she owned the world. "I'm hungry—and I want him to play another tune."

Shirl sat quietly, feeling, like Lin and Chris, a bit lost. It was like that game where you shut your eyes and two friends led you about by the hands. They could walk you in wide circles, tell you there were steps where there were none, spin you around and around, and you couldn't tell what was happening. You had to depend on your leaders. It was frightening sometimes. It was frightening now. She felt as if, after she had been led and spun for hours in the dark, her leader had left her in the middle of somewhere she didn't know—and she still couldn't open her eyes. It brought that kind of fear which takes your breath away and leaves your inside empty.

Mike felt a fool. Look how dark it was! His parents would be worrying and he'd missed his dinner. It would be baked when he got home to it, through being kept warm in the oven. Besides, he'd get a good clouting from his mother for staying out so late and frightening her— though why *she* should be frightened was a mystery. He couldn't think why he had followed the luchorpan at all . . . there was just something—way back in his mind,

47

drifting like smoke . . . if he could catch that thought and hold it, it would give him the answer. But the idea wasn't solid enough. It blew away like smoke.

The luchorpan, stepping fast and light across and over the common, never missing a step or noticing that the ground was uneven, was delighted with himself. He had his company for one thing, and he would need them. He had them all strongly tied by the ears and they would follow him anywhere. He could work at night now, when he was at his best.

Even the damage done to the country by the human-kind didn't seem so bad now. He could correct some of the mistakes they had made. Little things that wouldn't be noticed by anyone. He touched his hat respectfully, and then thought of the monkey-puzzle tree, and choked on a snigger. He began to whistle.

He came to a road and walked along it, not wishing to step on to the tarmac until he had to. He was looking for a house, any kind of house, and until he felt that one was near he walked on the grass. Then he dashed across the road in three steps, and back on to the grass, finally coming to a gap in the hedge and a notice. He couldn't read, but the track leading back from the gap looked suspiciously like a farm-track, and it was also going in the direction he would have to take anyway. This was just what he needed, and it proved that if you had faith you had no problems.

It *was* a farm-track, ending in a farm-yard in front of a farmhouse. This was wonderful. He could get food

48

from the farmhouse, and then go up to the stone, and *they'd* be waiting for him. He touched the brim of his hat again and strode boldly out across the yard.

He didn't care about the sudden chittering of the hens as they heard his steps, nor was he bothered when one of the pigs woke and began to snuffle, grunt and then scream. Once it became dark, he knew, the human kind didn't come out of their safe houses to meet the Little People, or something worse, that might be frightening the hens outside the door.

So he was a good deal shaken when the farmhouse door opened, letting an oblong of yellow light ripple over the yard's cobbles; and a big, thickly-made man stepped into the patch of light, with the top buttons of his shirt undone, and his trousers slung low. Mouth pressed into a hard line, he stared at Toole O'Dyna, luchorpan, for a few minutes, and then said, "What d'yer think yer doin', creepin' about me yard?"

The luchorpan, recovered from his surprise, lowered his head menacingly, and tried to outstare the man, looking up from under his brows. "Get back inside," he said, "if yer want luck on yer crops an' yer cattle."

The man's eyebrows lifted and he hissed through his teeth with exasperation. He said, "Get off me farm, chap, afore I put me boot under yer."

"I want food," the luchorpan told him. "Else I'll curse yer. Yer children'll sicken, born and unborn, yer crops'll be blighted, and yer cattle'll go lame an' die."

"Hey," growled the man. He pointed with one short, thick finger. "Watch it. If you want to frighten somebody with yer curses, go an' find some old lady, an' don't

49

come tryin' it on me. Yer liable to get yer head knocked off. Now get out of it."

The luchorpan didn't move, he couldn't believe that the man meant it. So the man came forward and Toole O'Dyna hurriedly went back, down the path and into the shadows. The man could not have been able to hurt him, but he was a big man and frightening.

The luchorpan crouched in the green coolness of the farm-track and waited until the farm was quiet again. He crept back to the yard, not so cocky this time, hushing the pigs and hens. But at the step he found no bowl of milk, no bread, no fruit, no ale put out to keep the Little People in a good mood.

He sat on his heels by the step, scowling blackly under his hat. His company had said that no one believed in elves any more, but he hadn't accepted that until now. There was only one thing to do. That was to go and ask for help. *They* might know of another house or farm who did believe in the Little People.

He got up and crept around the house. There were no lights on in any of the windows, for which he was thankful. He didn't particularly want to meet that farmer again.

Behind the house there were farrowing sheds and toilets, a brick stable and a barn. Then the fields. The luchorpan crossed them, going by the hedges, careful of the growing things, pushing through the field-dividing bushes until he came to land planted with beet. In the centre of the field was a small hill, wearing a fuzz of trees on its crown. He started out for the hill, threading through the rows of beet, climbing the bank, brushing through the nettles and ducking under branches. In the centre of the circlet of trees, at the very top of the hill, was a stone. Just one stone, pillar-like in shape, leaning a little now with the green moss climbing up it. The luchorpan reached out his hands and touched the stone, feeling the carvings that could no longer be seen. He leaned his body against the stone, felt its coldness against his cheek, closed his eyes and sank. Sank into the earth. Became stone.

There was no answer. After a moment he opened his eyes and pushed himself away from the stone with both hands. He frowned at it, puzzled, allowed his arms to bend so that he was flat against the stone once more. But there was nothing. The stone was neither dead nor alive—only vacant.

The luchorpan stepped back from the stone and stood staring at it. Had the human-kind destroyed even this? If they had, then he was entirely alone. Throughout the whole world he might be the only one of his kind—and he had no way of contacting the others. He thought of the Howe and of Aeve, and he felt very cold as he wondered if he were cut off from them for ever.

He stood there, perfectly still, for almost ten minutes, but then as a cool breeze rustled with the night through the leaves overhead, he grinned. He had his flute. He would find a way back to the Howe eventually. Sure he would. The human-kind didn't worry him, they were too stupid. And—if there was no one to help him, then there was no one to hinder him either. He could do anything he liked. He bit his thumb as he thought of what he could do.

As he passed the farmhouse on the way back, he carried trailing stems of honeysuckle and dog-rose, bindweed and ivy. He walked around the house, beginning with the right-hand side, and dropped one of the stems at each corner. He strolled over to the pig-run and leaned against the gate-post, lifted his whistle and began to play.

A fast tune with a fast rhythm, rising upwards, twisting and spiralling; and then heavy, humming, warm and thick. . . .

And when he had blown out the last, low note, he left, and the sound of leaf rubbing against leaf was loud behind him.

"But if you go," Lin wailed, "he'll be angry an' he won't play to us!"

"Play to you!" Mike said. "Play to you! I can't remember *any* of his playin'. Fine tunes they must be when yer can't remember 'em. I've got a home if you lot ain't, an' I'm goin' to it!"

"But if he plays again we'll be able to remember it this time," Shirl said happily. "We'll be able to sing it next time, maybe."

At her words a fear trickled down through Mike's chest, into his stomach ". . . be able to sing it. . . ." Why should that sound so terrible? "I'm goin' home," he said hastily. "There's footer on the telly tonight." He bounced his ball and caught it to underline his words.

"Footer! Telly!" Chris said, with un-Chris like fierceness.

"You're frightened," Lin sneered, screwing her face up. "Goin' to run home to yer Mom?"

Mike didn't like Linda. She always complained, always whined, always took the mickey in that creeping way. He found defence in attack. "If you'd got any sense you'd go home too, only you ain't so you don't."

"Why don't yer go then?" Lin asked. "We don't want yer. Is it 'cos yer frightened to walk home in the dark by yerself?"

"I'd be a damn sight more frightened if I had to walk home with you!" Mike told her. "Frankenstein's monster's got nothin' on you!"

"Oh, shut yer faces!" Shirl said to anyone who was listening.

They should have known by this sudden outbreak of ill feeling that the luchorpan was near. He came through the trees just as Mike turned to leave.

"I'm goin' home," he announced to the luchorpan.

"Have yer got anythin' to eat?" Lin asked, almost at the same moment as Shirl called, "Will yer play us a tune?"

"I will, I will," the luchorpan said quickly, dropping into the hollow. "I couldn't get any food, but I'll play a tune, I will. Mike, Mick, Mickeen, will yer not stay an' hear the tune, only stay an' hear the tune I'll play yer...."

"I want to go home," Mike said stubbornly, and began to walk away.

"Go home, go home, but stay an' hear the tune first. It won't hurt to hear the tune, it won't hurt, Mickeen, only to hear the tune, it'll make the way back go quicker. Hear the tune, an' *then* go home."

There was something in Mike's mind; perhaps it was the call of the twentieth century through football and the telly, or perhaps something older; but it struck over and over again: Don't listen, don't listen, don't listen— like a bell.

Mike said, "I don't know."

"Aah, come on now, Mickeen, be the brave man! A little tune hurt yer? Only music? How could it hurt yer at all? Only stay and hear the tune, then go home. . . ."

Mike squeezed his eyes shut so that spots whirled away from them when he opened them again. He tried to shut his ears to the luchorpan's voice, and the one bright, high note that he blew on his whistle; but it was impossible unless he stuck a finger in each ear, and that would look babyish. There was another handful of flute notes, falling as if they had been dropped; so penetrating that they would have reached Mike even if he had been stone deaf.

"All right," Mike said, and the bell in his head rose to a great clamour. "Only a tune," the luchorpan soothed, as he moved towards the yellow fire. "Only a tune."

He sat with the others in the firelight, while Mike stood with the dark and the trees.

The music came, a crooning, crooning tune, a mother's chanted, senseless lullaby, a rocking tune, rocking like a sea of milk, rocking and rocking, creeping among the trees of the hollow like mist, and the listeners swayed to it slowly, easily, feeling warm and drowsy, feeling wrapped in warm wool on a cold day, surrounded by the fire's yellow light which kept them away from the dark and cold, and all trouble. . . .

Mike, in the darkness, was fish-cold—his mind seemed to have icicles driving into it. He clung to the straight and still trunk of a tree with both arms and pressed himself against it. He knew clearly that he must keep still and awake, not listen to the music . . . but it was difficult to resist when he was already so tired and cold. The tune plainly begged him to sleep, promised him comfort and happiness, almost patted his shoulder. And when the tune began to fall asleep, with heavy eyes and pleasant dozing, then Mike fell with it.

The luchorpan walked over to him and bent, watching his face. He blew another string of notes, quiet, stroking, easy-breathing notes, smiled, put the whistle away and squatted beside the boy as he checked the distance between them and the fire with his eyes. Then he laid his hand on Mike's shoulder, palm flat, fingers lifted slightly upwards. His mouth was pulled into an 'o' as he concentrated, pressing down on his palm. Then he lifted his hand up, and Mike came with it, still in his sleeping position, as if lying on the air. The luchorpan came fully to his feet and walked to the fire, Mike floating with him, attached to his hand. At the fire the luchorpan bent again, bringing Mike back to the ground. It took a little time to break the hold, to ease his palm away from Mike's shoulder, and then he could move away from the fire, which he had made for his company's comfort, and sit in the dark.

He cursed himself quietly for a fool. All that trouble! He'd nearly lost the most important one, only because

55

he'd thought the other tunes were strong enough to hold them. Well—they were for the other three, but not for that Mike, and what would the use of it be without that Mike? He should have seen that he had a stronger mind than the others and . . . but he relaxed. Why make a noise now? He'd played Forgetfulness, and in the morning, they would all have forgotten the time before they met him—even Mike. So the danger was over. He lay back with his arms behind his head, and his knees bent up, and grinned at the trees above him.

His thoughts slipped back to the stone, and how there had been no answer for him. Where were *they*? He thought that they might have given Earth up for a bad job. Serve the human-kind right. Teach 'em not to worship false gods. But by the Old One, he was going to enjoy himself now. He'd make the human-kind jump! And they'd have no one to complain to about him. . . . He put one ankle up on the other knee and began to whistle as he swung the foot up and down.

Chapter 6

On Sunday morning Mrs. Surrel heard a knock on the kitchen door, and left her flower-arranging to answer it. It was Mr. Runley, the man who came three days a week to keep the garden in good shape. He was an old ruffian, Mrs. Surrel thought, as he leant there, with one hand on the wall; the lower part of his face bristling with white hair, his broken nose red where it spread below his little, wicked, blue eyes, and his black, ancient working jacket slipping off one hunched, bear-like shoulder.

"Good morning, Mr. Runley," she said.

He snuruffled loudly up his nose, wiped it on the back of one large, brown hand, gave his roaring smoker's cough, and said, "Afternoon more like. The monkey-puzzle tree's jed. I've come to tell. . . ."

She had translated 'jed' into 'dead', and now asked, "You mean the Chilean Pine?"

"I mean the monkey-puzzle." He was a man who had no use for fancy names. "It's as jed as a door stop. 'Twas all right Thursdee an' all. So I've come for a bowl o' milk an' a platter o' bread."

'I've come for. . . .' Mrs. Surrel noted, not, 'Please may I have. . . .' or even 'I've come to ask for. . . .' He was very impolite. But she only said, though coldly, "Whatever do you want those for?"

"To put by monkey-puzzle tree!" he said, angry, because he was impatient. His shaggy eyebrows jumped, and his eyes flashed bright. He roared and growled with coughing again.

"To put by the tree?" Mrs. Surrel said. "I'm sorry, but I don't understand, Mr. Runley. I can't see that any purpose would be served by putting milk and bread by the tree." But as she said it, she thought that perhaps bread and milk was some old gardener's cure for dead monkey-puzz—Chilean Pines.

Runley was staring at her from under his eyebrows with fierce blue eyes. He counted the points which he wished her to understand on enormous, strong fingers. "The monkey-puzzle tree's jed! It was all right on Thursdee! So I want a bowl o' milk an' a platter o' bread!"

"I'm sorry, Mr. Runley," Mrs. Surrel said, with alarming politeness, "but I haven't so much bread and milk that I can spare some for trees."

"Yo put some bread an' milk out, he'll leave thee be!" scowled Mr. Runley.

"Who will?" asked Mrs. Surrel in surprise.

"*He* will. *Him* as killed the monkey-puzzle."

Mrs. Surrel gathered her light and lacy cardigan about her, and bustled past him down the path. "Has someone chopped it down?" she cried.

It hadn't been chopped down. It had been blasted. Most of it was useless even for kindling wood. What was left was well and truly dead, scorched and twisted.

Mrs. Surrel goggled at it. The tree might have been struck by a particularly vicious stroke of lightning, except that there had been no lightning for months. She could think of nothing to say.

"*He* killed it," Tom Runley said, standing beside her like a heap of old rags. "When I seed this mess here, I ses to meself, I know *him* for what he is. They ain't good, Missis, say what thee'd a mind, they ain't good. They'm evil. Wicked they am. An' if *I* was thee, knowin' what I know, I'd get some bread an' milk out fast, wheer he'll find it. He might let thee be then."

"For goodness sake, talk sense!" Mrs. Surrel snapped. She was ruffled by the sight of the inexplicably damaged tree.

"I am talkin' sense," Tom said, "for them as have sense. Them as hain't, won't see sense in owt. I'm tellin' thee, there's an elf about, an' if he's the one I think he is, we'm in for trouble."

"A—an elf!" Mrs. Surrel choked. She looked at the tree, which had been smashed without any sound or sign. She thought of the books she had in the house, books of fairy tales, legends, folk-lore, and magic. She was deeply interested in the subject, but had always treated it as that—a subject. Stories, myths, not reality. To stand in her own garden, in front of her mysteriously murdered Chilean Pine, and to have such a down-to-earth, practical man as Tom Runley tell her that an elf had done the foul deed was *like* a fairy tale in itself.

"But—an elf!" she said.

"Please theesen then, Missis," Tom said. "If I was thee I'd have milk an' bread out here so fast me feet wouldn't touch the floor. It should be pasteurised milk out a fat bottle, if thee've got it, and brown bread." He went off, coughing, to the tiny, neat, rose-grown tool-shed at the bottom of the garden.

Mrs. Surrel tottered back to the house.

When Shirl awoke from her sleep in the hollow, it was daylight, and there was only the cottony sound of a football being kicked beyond the trees. She sat up, blinking a little, sleepy, but not hungry, or stiff, or cold. The fire was still burning, its yellow primrose in the daylight. None of the branches had been burnt away, the fire was just burning on them. There was a great deal of smoke about, filling the hollow, very thick and strangely greenish, as if they were under water.

Lin sat up and asked, "Is there anything to eat?"

"I don't think so," Shirl told her. "Why? Are yer hungry? I ain't."

Lin thought about it, and then said that she wasn't, not really. Mike grumbled at them to hush up and let other folks get some sleep.

Shirl, looking round for the luchorpan, didn't see him at first, because he was lying away from the fire, with his hat over his eyes, one arm tidily across his chest, the other flung out to the side. She pointed him out to Lin. "Ask him if yer really want somethin' to eat."

Lin snorted in disgust. "He's never any use!"

The luchorpan rolled up on one elbow, holding his hat to shadow his eyes. "What's that?" he asked. "Who's without use?"

"She didn't mean it, Mr. Toole," Shirl said quickly. Then, after a pause, "What are we goin' to do today?"

"Do? Do?" the luchorpan groaned. "Aah, do what yer've a mind. Do anythin' yer like but don't bother me. Only don't go past the trees! Do yer hear me? Don't go past the trees, or b' th' Old One, I'll have yer guts for me garters!"

All four of them, Shirl, Lin and the boys who were just getting up, had heard this threat many times before, but none had, until now, heard it said as if it was meant.

"No, we won't, Mr. Toole," Shirl said timidly.

The luchorpan grinned at them and nodded, sat up and felt in his pocket. He pulled out his penny-whistle and threw it to Shirl, making it bounce off her head before it fell to the ground. "Try yer hands wi' that," he said, "while I'm sleepin' the sleep o' the good and the dead." He pointed a finger suddenly. "Gaah, but if yer so much as scratch paint off it, dead or alive, I'll make yer suffer, so I will! I've a great likin' for that whistle!"

He lay down, turned over, and then jumped up again. "One thing!" he said. "Get some branches, lots of 'em, an' pile 'em all up. I need 'em." And then he lay down again, and pulled his hat over his eyes, and left them looking at the whistle.

It was funny that they'd never really noticed it before. Long and slender it was, green with black bands. Ordinary. Very unmagical. But Shirl put her hands behind her. She wasn't going to touch it.

Mike picked it up first, with gentle fingers. He blew into it, his eyes staring out over the top. A thin, scratchy note came out. Mike was surprised. He had blown it just as he had seen the luchorpan do—and the luchorpan's music didn't sound like that.

"You have to put your fingers over the holes," Lin said.

So Mike covered some of the holes, and blew again, and a sound came out that would have stampeded a herd of elephants. Mike dropped the whistle, and Shirl jumped. Chris and the girls began to laugh.

Mike turned red and shouted at Chris, "You play it then! You're so clever!" He shoved the whistle into Chris's hand.

"Careful!" Shirl said nervously.

Chris had had some recorder lessons at school. A recorder wasn't the same as a penny-whistle, but he could have a go. He produced three or four tin-whistley sounds, scratchy, shrill and unpleasant, before taking the pipe from his mouth and having a closer look.

"It's different," he said. "I mean, it's different from a whistle an' everythin'." The others didn't know anything about musical instruments, tin whistles or recorders, and so they hadn't noticed what Chris noticed now.

There were more holes than there should have been. He had never seen a whistle like this one before, but surely it shouldn't have—two, four—ten, twelve—thirteen holes. And some of the holes were at the sides of the pipe, and three were arranged in a triangle just below the mouth-piece. "I can't play this," Chris said. "I don't see how anybody can."

"*He* does," Lin said reasonably, nodding towards the sleeping—if he was sleeping—luchorpan. She took the whistle from Chris and turned it about, so that the black bands on it seemed to twist like a turning spiral. She put it to her mouth and blew gently and there came a most eerie, stealthy noise, like leaves rustling, or something creeping. Lin hastily passed the whistle on to Shirl, who wanted nothing to do with it, and gave it back to Mike. Mike wasn't going to show himself up again. He put it down on the grass and reminded them of the luchorpan's orders to collect branches.

"Don't know what he wants them for, though," he said. "Fire don't seem to be burnin' 'em, do it?"

It was while they were hunting through long grass and leaf-mould for fallen branches, and struggling to pull down live ones, that a football came flying through the trees and bounced on the ground in the hollow. Mike started for it, to kick it back, but before he could reach it a boy sprang over the bank through the trees, hot, red in the face, arms and legs splaying out in all directions as he ran.

"I got it!" he shouted breathlessly, scooped up the ball and hurried back again, partly running, partly walking, partly jumping. Mike looked at the others wide-eyed. The boy hadn't seen them. He had squarely faced Mike over the ball and had not seen him.

Mike went to the edge of the trees, and peered out. There were five boys with the football, one in goal and two teams of two, to kick the ball into the goal, and to keep it out. He shouted to attract their attention. They didn't hear. He thought that they should have heard, because his voice sounded loud enough to himself. It was a bit like losing your voice, and not knowing. He thought about going nearer and shouting once more, but that meant going outside the trees; and when the luchorpan had threatened to take their guts for garters he had said it in a tone that Mike would remember for a very long time.

He turned back into the hollow, and swung about, looking sourly at everything and everyone. Then he said suddenly, "It's that green smoke that does it. Betcha. Bet yer anythin'." He pointed at the luchorpan. "He's a crafty monkey-pig, ain't he?"

They nodded. Chris had the whistle again, trying to play it. But with all the holes and their baffling positions, he felt that he needed another finger or two. He could only make weird noises come out, peepings and booms, thuds and scrapings.

Mike was scooping up dirt and piling it on to the fire, trying to put it out. But the yellow flames were completely indifferent to him. Since they weren't burning the branches, but only burning on them, they could burn on dirt just as well. Mike sat back on his heels. "Cuss and blind!" he said angrily. "Cuss an' cuss."

The only answer he got was a choked gurgling from the whistle as Chris covered another set of holes and blew down it.

When the luchorpan woke it was smoky-dark, and they were all delighted, because they were so bored. They watched him eagerly as he stood up and dusted himself with both hands, shook his hat, and came to the fire, silently holding out a hand. After a moment or two, Chris placed the whistle in the hand, and the fingers closed over it. The luchorpan threw the pipe up and caught it again.

"Enjoy yerselves?" he asked.

"Yes," Shirl said untruthfully, but no one else answered.

"Please, Mr. Toole, sir," Chris burst out, "how do yer play it with all them holes? I mean, there's some on the side an' that, how do yer . . . ?"

The luchorpan grinned, put the whistle in his mouth and clasped both hands at the back of his neck. He marched up and down playing a tune that had no tune, but only made pictures in the listeners' heads. Pictures of the sun, and light, and daytime. Just before the end the unheard music dropped into a warmer song and a face floated for a second at the back of their eyes. A pointed, smiling, dark and lovely face—but the luchorpan stopped playing with a jerk, and the face disappeared. It came and went so quickly that they hardly remembered it.

"That was music of the better class," said the luchorpan, after a moment's silence. "Yer know how it's played now, do yer not?"

"No," Chris admitted. "You didn't play it with your fingers at all that time."

"Oh, he's a sharp one," said the luchorpan, shaking his head in wonderment. "When a brick wall falls on that one, sure he notices it straight away. Did yer get them branches?"

Mike pointed to the heap of branches they had collected and piled to one side. The luchorpan grinned again and gathered up an armful of the bigger ones. "Come on," he said. "Bring the rest."

They did, wondering what he wanted with a lot of branches, and followed him through the trees and out on to the open common, crossing the lumpy paths made by cars, and tripping once more in the dusk.

The branches were laid down on the tired grass, in a spot where no heather grew, and they stood around, shivering and hopping, watching the elf. He was taking the branches, one by one, standing them upright and driving them into the ground, so that they stuck up on their own. He placed them in a large circle. Shirl went to help him, because she was cold doing nothing.

"What are you doing now?" Chris asked, as he too came to lend a hand.

"Aah, a wonderful thing," replied the luchorpan lightly.

The circle was completed, only needed a bit of rearranging. They stood, arms wrapped around themselves, as the luchorpan took out his whistle, smiling to himself, nodding his head in time to music that only he could hear. Ready, he began to play, to walk round and around the circle with the tune breaking like icicles into the cold air. It was a soft, pulling call to awaken something that didn't want to wake, with the luchorpan walking solemnly round. The call came again and a shudder that wasn't caused by cold ran down Shirl's back. She felt a pulling too, inside her, as if she were wool and were being unravelled.

"Don't he look daft?" Mike asked, but the others hissed angrily at him to shut up.

The tune's call ended, and a story began. A story of trees. Saplings, thin and whippy, that strengthened into young trees, and grew into thick, ivy-cloaked oaks. Trees that towered thick, never ending, across the country with no one to cut them down, no one who dared to cut them down. Men dying and being forgotten, men's huts changing from wattle to brick, but still the trees, night and day—until man got too powerful.

The others didn't notice, it seemed natural to them, they even expected it; but Mike, in a dreamlike far-away sort of mood, saw the branches of the circle thicken and jump up, grow bushy with leaves. And then he heard the tune again, with its story of the oak's endless strength, and it seemed to him that there was nothing more ordinary than that the branches should grow into trees.

The luchorpan was moving away from the circle now, and his tune became faster and faster. Where he trod the grass was coming up greener and thicker, and saplings followed him, saplings that with the speed of the music sprang up into huge trees in a few minutes. They ran after him in a fright that he would get so far ahead that the music would fade away; and where they ran more new grass came, and saplings, more and more trees. Where Lin dragged her hand across a trunk, ivy grew, twining upwards about the tree. Where Shirl touched the wood, mistletoe crept out from the bark. Toadstools scattered from Chris's feet, moss fled across the damp ground from Mike's, to scurry up the trees.

The forest grew up around them, dense and almost trackless, as it had been eight centuries before. The light faded to greenness and quietness came. It was beautiful. All the time the tune was reaching down into their minds and searching—and what was a car anyway? Or a bus? Or an aeroplane?

Shirl found that her shoes were cramping her feet,

making them hot. She dropped down, pulled off the shoes, threw them away—and they disappeared. Shoes like that didn't exist in a medieval forest.

She ran to catch up with the others, the grass cool beneath her feet and between her toes. Ahead the music still told its tale of trees.

Chapter 7

On Monday morning Col Davies came out of his house while it was still dark. He walked, head down, collar turned up against the cold, rainy mist. But somehow things were different. He didn't look up from the herring-boned garden path below him, but he could feel that things were different. The countryside felt closer. The dark shadows fell wrongly, and the slight grey light fell on his little garden, his path, his rain barrel, in the wrong pattern. He glanced up, eyes squinting in his brown face and he stopped.

He stopped dead and stood, his eyes opening up from their squint, his lips slowly parting in disbelief. He stared and stared and all the time his mind muttered to him that he was not seeing what his eyes were seeing.

Away across the country, where the common had been, there was now a thick, solid wall of trees. Right across they stretched, as far as the Portway ridge, blue in the distance, and away towards the horizon in the other direction. A few of the trees had crept out from the general mass like scouts. One was a little way down the road, growing in the hedge, a huge oak tree, hundreds of years old, that hadn't been there the night before.

They were only trees. His muscles eased a little, he drew in a long breath, felt his heart start again with a rattle and a jump, felt his belly tremble like a jelly. Only trees. He crept towards the gate, heading for his work at the Devilstun Farm. He reached out a hand for the gate-latch, and saw a dog in the road outside.

It was a very big dog, shaggy and grey. Green eyes, long teeth. In fact, it wasn't a dog at all, Col thought calmly, hand still on the latch. He had been to the Zoo with his wife and kids, had read the little label on the cage that listed the Latin name, habits and habitat of the grey wolf. Col turned and ran back to his door, crashed against the wood, fumbling for his key, fell into the kitchen where his wife had not yet gone back to bed. She was surprised, wouldn't believe him until she had looked for herself. Then she shut the door and bolted it.

The news of the overnight forest was brought back to Halmsbury by a lorry-driver who had been travelling along a road to work when the tarmac had vanished into a crush of trees. Later people tried to get to work in cars, but most had to turn back, and try to get out of the town by another way. In a very short time a reporter from the 'Halmsbury Telephone' was out at what had been the common, taking dozens of photographs and writing down the remarks of the local people in a little note-book. He got the story of Col Davies' shock and the wolf, and at mid-day he dropped into a little pub called the 'Green Man' for a pint and a cheese-and-tomato sandwich. One of the men already there, a

70

grubby-looking old rogue with an unshaven face and a broken red nose, began to talk.

" 'Course I know all about it," he said, and sniffed, waiting.

"Get away, Tom," Col Davies said without enthusiasm. Col was in the pub recovering from severe shock.

"It's an elf," Tom said decidedly, "as is playin' his whistle an' makin' the trees come."

"Aah, get away, Tom," said Col again.

"You can laugh!" Tom shouted. "You can laugh all you've a mind, but I dain't plant them trees, did I? Nor none o' you lot dain't neither. An' they dain't just come by theirsen, for no reason."

There was complete, heavy-breathing silence, and then a lot of coughing, sliding of beer-glasses up and down, a scratching of heads, a stretching of bottom lips. Col Davies stared at Tom with rapt attention.

Tom smiled and took a swig of beer. "Me Great, Great, Great Gran'ferther," he began, "his name was Caleb Runley. He was alive when they was diggin' the cuts, only a kid he was. He remembered an' told me Great, Great Gran'ferther, who told me Great Gran'ferther, who told me Gran'ferther, who told me ferther, who told me. He said how they found an elf amongst the navvies who was workin' on the cut. They was Irish, some on 'em, an' this was an Irish elf. He worked a lot of trouble, so Caleb said, sourin' milk, skimmin' milk, lamin' cattle and bringin' the sides o' the cut in. But the Irish liked him, always tipped their caps to him, so Caleb said, always saved a bit of anythin' they had nice for him. An' Caleb noticed as nothin' ever

71

happened to the Irish navvies. Caleb must have been a noticin' sort of lad. He said nobody ever noticed, bar hisself, how the ones that got the troubles was the ones that made trouble for the elf an' his mates. He said that the farmer as used to give 'em butter-milk and sell 'em bread cheap never had a better year for his corn. Anyway, so Caleb said, they all took off after that elf, all the folks he'd worked trouble for, took off after him with holy water an' prayer books. They got a Catholic priest to put the fear o' Christ into the Irish navvies, so they was scared for their souls, an' they all went with the English after the elf. Caleb went along, he wanted to see what'd happen. He said that the elf run—so far. Then all the men comes tearin' down the slope, out on the common, an' the elf had stopped at the bottom of th' hill, just over a stream, an' he was waitin' for 'em. So o' course, they all stops, an' runs into one another, an' falls over, 'cos they was all frightened o' this elf really, an' they was waitin' for the priest. Well, the priest comes up, an' he starts rantin' on about goin' in God's name, O creature of darkness an' I don't know what, but the elf just laughs at him, an' the Irish am gettin' very restless, an' that got the priest worried. He takes out his bottle o' holy water, pulls out the cork, goin' to throw it at the elf, but all that comes out is steam, an' the elf's a-rollin' and laughin' on t'other side stream. Well then, so Caleb ses, one o' the Irish navvies cheers the elf—M'raw, or Murrough, or somethin' like that this navvy's name was—an' a fight started between the Irish and the English. An' when they'd finished the elf was gone an' the navvy who'd cheered was dead. Well, everybody'd got a good idea who'd killed him—a farm-hand called Slater—but he wouldn't admit it, an' none o' the others'd tell on him. So this Slater got away with it. Well, they all goes off, but some o' the Irish comes back later on to collect the body, but when they gets to where they'd left it, it ain't there, an' they never did find it as far as I know. An' Caleb never said nothin' about the elf comin' back either. But I reckon he's come back now, an' he's in a wicked mood, I'll be bound. Wicked an' evil." Tom leaned forward and rolled his eyes frighteningly at the men who had trickled out of the little inner room to listen. "Come back for his revenge!" he snarled. He took a long drink to loosen his throat after all that talking, while they gawped at him.

"Tom, what should us do?" Col Davies asked.

Tom smiled. He had won. "Accordin' to what Caleb said, yer should hang a branch of rowan tree over yer door, an' put some bread an' milk, or a bit of summat else out on the step. He'll do yer a good turn then, maybe, instead of a bad 'un."

Rosalyn Elmfield was late in arriving at school on Monday and had barely enough time to collect her class for the assembly. After assembly she had to drag them through an arithmetic lesson which she hated as much as they did. When she got to the Staff-room at break, she had forgotten all about the photograph she had in her bag.

There was a much more important subject being discussed. Mr. Colly, who taught the class below Miss

Elmfield's, was passing a newspaper around. It carried a story about four children who were missing from their homes. They all attended Halmsbury Primary School—this one—and they had all been missing since Saturday. They were believed to be together. Their names were: Linda Windmore, Shirley Plummer, Christopher Russel, and Michael Slater. The police would be interested to hear from anyone who had seen the children on Saturday morning or afternoon.

"Oh!" Miss Elmfield said, and everyone looked at her.

"I haven't seen them myself," she explained quickly. "But my aunt did. On Saturday morning. She saw them outside the museum with a man, and she took a photograph of them."

"That's good!" Mr. Colly said. "You want to take that photograph along to the police as soon as you can. It'll help them no end. If they've gone off with some man, I mean. Not just a vague description, but a photograph of him!"

Miss Elmfield was rattling furiously through the clutter in her handbag. "It's not like that at all," she stammered. "I don't think it'd be any help to the police. I brought it today because it's so odd. Oh—here it is——" She held it for them to see, particulary Mr. Colly.

Mr. Colly frowned at the photograph, then took it from her, and sat on the edge of his chair, looking at it, the newspaper hanging from his hand. He couldn't understand, at first, just how the white patch fitted into the picture. Then he said, "Now, how did that happen?"

"It's very strange, isn't it?" Miss Elmfield said, while everyone else hummed and hahhed. "Mr. Hadley—he

74

develops my aunt's photographs for her—he said that it was a trick of the light—or something."

Mr. Colly pressed up his mouth, then shook his head. "Tricks of light don't look like that," he said decidedly. "A trick of the light wouldn't blot one figure out like that, with no blurring or distortion."

"Perhaps the film was damaged," someone suggested.

"Or there could have been dust on the camera lens," said cheerful Mr. Chattem.

"My aunt said that the man—who should be where the white patch is—was dressed in old-fashioned clothes," Miss Elmfield said. "Now she thinks he's a leprechaun."

She saw Mr. Colly's hand, holding the photograph, jump, and she wondered why.

"It could be a fault in your camera," Mr. Pittal said.

"Oh no," Miss Elmfield said. "The camera was new. It wouldn't have gone wrong already."

Mr. Colly was shaking his head. "It wouldn't matter anyway," he said. "You're just making excuses for something you can't understand. Dust on the lens! Damaged film, camera gone wrong! I'm almost certain that none of these things would make a camera produce a picture like this. Look—the white is the shape of a man. The outline's clear, no blurs, no rough edges."

No one said anything for quite a few seconds.

"What can have caused it then?" asked Mr. Pittal. "You tell us."

"I don't know." Mr Colly waved a hand. "I can't give an explanation for everything. I just know that none of your explanations are good enough. I can only say that there was a person there—a man—who, for

75

some reason, hasn't shown on the film. Perhaps he was a ghost."

There was a slight giggle, and Miss Elmfield told him, "That's just what I said."

But Mr. Colly was frowning at the titterers. "What's funny?" he demanded. "I'm not joking. Why shouldn't he be a ghost? Why shouldn't he, eh? It explains things a darn sight better than dust on the lens!" He saw protest coming, and silenced it with, "Don't tell me that there's no such things as ghosts! Tell me instead why there shouldn't be!"

It was a difficult challenge to meet. While Mr. Colly was waiting the bell rang for the end of break.

"Let's reason it out," he said, ignoring the bell. "This man—he's short, isn't he? Well, he must be a solid, 'real'—er—being—for a start. Because, you see, if he were invisible, you'd be able to see the children and the wall and everything through him. But this man has just blocked it all out. So we've got that he must be solid."

The others waited, in baffled, or amused, silence.

"But—" Mr. Colly went on, "but—although he's solid, he doesn't show on the film. The film won't take him, the camera won't—won't admit him—to be there. So he can't be human. . . ." He shook his head. "I don't know. Maybe he's one of the Little People. Did any of that make sense?"

"No," Mr. Pittal said.

"If it can't be proved with a bunsen-burner and a test-tube your mind can't take in it," Mr. Colly retorted.

"You can't be serious though," Miss Elmfield said.

Mr. Colly smiled sheepishly, "I don't know, I don't know." His hands waved, fingers outspread, as he searched for words. "Listen," he said. "It's been the fashion for the last hundred years or so to say that ghosts don't exist, and that they're in the same class as dragons and—and long-legged beasties, things that go bump in the night—and fairies. But before that people had always believed in these things—well, ghosts and fairies anyhow—and—left to themselves, without scientists and that—*everyone* believes in ghosts nowadays. Deep down. When they admit it to themselves. There aren't many people that feel quite safe at night—though why we should be more frightened of dead people than we are of living ones I don't know. But look—this is what I'm trying to say—even if ghosts are a legend now, there must have been *something* to start the legend, because people believe in ghosts all over the world, Eskimoes, Aborigines, Red Indians—everybody. And if there are ghosts—and there's evidence for their existence—then why not Little People? That's another 'legend' that people all over the world believe in. Why not a race of people who aren't quite the same as us? Who don't work to quite the same rules? Why not? And there are still places, you know—not in darkest Africa, or Outer Mongolia either—in countries like Ireland and England—where people always take their hats off to the fairies as they pass a certain spot, and won't go to other places after dark. But those same people will tell you that there are no such things as fairies—because the scientists have got at them, and they know that they aren't supposed to believe in fairies. It's a sort of instinct, you know, and

77

instinct about fairies and ghosts goes deeper than what you're taught."

"I think I see what you mean," Miss Elmfield said.

"That's more than I do," said Mr. Pittal. "And meanwhile the sweet little kiddies we are paid to teach are tearing the school down. And you've forgotten all about those missing children in the fury of the debate." He bent over Miss Elmfield. "If I were you I'd 'phone the police straight away and tell them about this man."

"It was my aunt who saw him, actually," Miss Elmfield said.

"Well, I don't suppose the police would mind hearing from your aunt as well, but I think you should tell them as soon as possible."

"I will—if you think so," Miss Elmfield said, getting up to go to the telephone.

It was strange, she thought, that two such different people had come to the same conclusion about the man outside the museum. Her Aunt Virginia had said he was a leprechaun, but her Aunt Virginia was a silly little woman. But Mr. Colly had followed a logical argument—well, he thought it logical, and it sounded temptingly so—and then had said "Maybe he's one of the Little People."

Her mind, her educated, school-teacher mind, tried to prove Mr. Colly's argument silly, but found itself in knots. Something underneath her mind agreed with him.

Chapter 8

Tom Runley, waiting at the bus-stop, watched the man coming along the road. He knew that the man would wait at the bus-stop because he knew the man. Not his name, but he had seen him about and spoken to him. Tom didn't think much of him either—he was one of them school teacher fellers. Dead ignorant. Knowed nothin'. But he was somebody to talk to.

" 'Ternoon," Tom said, as the man stopped. "Gooin' on all right?"

"Oh—yes. I'm all right. How are you?" Mr. Colly asked in return, politely. He knew Tom in much the same way as Tom knew him.

"Good as ever I was," Tom said, feeling in the pocket of his ancient wrinkled trousers for a cigarette.

There was a silence while he searched for his matches, lit one and put the flame to his cigarette. Then he said, "Some fine gooin's on at your school."

Mr. Colly made a noise that could have meant yes or no.

"What I kip wonderin'," went on Tom, "is what he wants them kids for."

Mr. Colly's ears twitched. "Kids?" he said. "What kids?"

"Them four as am missin'," Tom said scornfully, telling himself that he was right about the teacher's stupidity. "'S all over the papers this mornin'. Thee don't notice much, dost?"

Mr. Colly ignored the insult and asked eagerly, "You know something about the children?" Tom smiled, looking villainous with his stubbled face and broken nose. "I know more than most," he said.

"You'd better tell the police then, hadn't you?" Mr. Colly said sternly, "Instead of boasting about it. *Have* you told the police?"

Tom gave him a withering look as he blew smoke out of his mouth. He said slowly, "If I told the police about *him*, they'd have me inside afore me feet touched the floor." He tapped his head. "They'd think I was nuts."

Mr. Colly looked at the man, and then looked all about him. He moved closer. "Why?" he whispered.

Tom gave him another sneering glance. "'Cos they don't b'lieve in elves, yer big Ayli-Tooli," he said, loud enough to be heard at the other end of the street.

"Do you believe in elves?" Mr Colly asked.

"I do. I've always said so straight out. It's an elf as has took them kids—for purposes of his own," he added darkly.

And then Mr. Colly opened his mouth and told Tom all about the photograph which Miss Elmfield's aunt had taken. Tom nodded, and listened, and threw ash about, and then took Mr. Colly by the arm, turned him about and walked him off down the road, "Bus'll be comin' soon," he said, "an we can't talk about elves on buses. There's some very funny women get on buses.

Listen. I do gardenin' for this woman, Surrel her name is, an' her's got this monkey-puzzle tree. . . ."

"A what?"

"Chilly pine her calls it, but it's a monkey-puzzle just the same."

"I've never heard of a Chilly Pine either," Mr. Colly said.

"Aah, yer've seen 'em about. Skinny, ugly-lookin' things they are, all covered in spikes. I was up her house Sunday an' her monkey-puzzle was all in rags; I ses to meself, that ain't natural-like, what can have done it?"

He paused for breath, and Mr. Colly asked, "You mean that an elf had—destroyed—the tree?"

"No. I mean *the* elf, the one that's loose. An' it's like I said to Mrs. Surrel, if he's the one I think he is, we'm in for trouble 'cos he's a right little bleeder. But listen— I was up Devilstun way this afternoon, 'cos I know a feller up theer—a farmer. But—this is the thing—he hears me comin' up the path in me van an' he comes to meet me with his dogs an' his shot-gun. 'Tom, Tom,' he ses, 'I'm ruddy glad to see it's thee. Tom, I'm unnerved, I am unnerved.'" He gave Mr. Colly a dramatic and meaningful look from under shaggy, fierce eyebrows. "Unnerved he said he was. I ses, 'Thee look it, owd mate,' I ses, 'What's up?' 'Come an' see,' he ses, an' I went with him an' his house! His house! It was just covered all over wi' growin' plants—ivy an' trumpet flowers an' all that sort of thing, yer know. He said it had took since Sundee mornin' to cut his way out wi' the carvin' knife. Like the Amazonian jungles, he said it was, like slashin' yer way through Amazonian jungles. He ses a

81

gypsy feller had come round beggin', an' when he couldn't get nothin' he tried to frighten him with curses. Well, he wouldn't like that, this feller, so he told him to clear off afore he put his boot under him, an' now he ses the gypsy's curses am comin' true, 'cos his wife an' daughter am sick, an' he'd just checked his cattle an' each an' every one on 'em was lame. Proper unnerved he was. But I ses to myself, Tom, I ses, thee know better. He was an elf, I ses to meself, an' God help us all."

Mr. Colly was silent for a while, taking all this in. At last he asked quietly, "What should one do?"

His companion guffawéd deep in his chest. "What? About the elf? 'One' should do nowt, I reckon. Keep clear of him."

"But what about the children?"

"Aah, he won't hurt them. They'm probably happier wi' him than they am at home, ungrateful little oojars."

Mr. Colly was shocked. "But you can't leave them like that! I mean—if—if the elf isn't human you can't tell what he might do!"

"He won't hurt 'em. He'll look after 'em."

"But—but what has he taken them for, then? I thought they didn't like us. . . ."

Tom looked at him with disgust. "Power!" he said. "When he's got the kids with him he's stronger."

Mr. Colly made two telephone calls that evening—one to Miss Elmfield and one to a Mrs. Surrel.

Mrs. Surrel's house wasn't really very large, but it

seemed so, and Mrs. Surrel herself seemed bigger than she really was. She had that towering stiffness of figure that means tight corsets. She wore high-heeled shoes, too, and a puffed-up-on-top hair-style. But the biggest thing about her was her sweet kindness. It oozed all over you, set hard about you like melted sugar, and seemed as ready to crack.

When Mr. Colly and Miss Elmfield arrived, she fussed them into the living-room, and asked them to sit down; and she fussed her husband and son away to some hidey-hole she had for them. Next she switched off the television and shut it into its case, smiled upon them, and steered her stiff and dignified way into the kitchen. She was back inside ten minutes, with tiny green and gold cups of instant coffee on green and gold saucers with frilled edges. Also a larger, matching plate of assorted biscuits. Mr. Colly sat uncomfortably in his chair, holding his cup and saucer high so that his arm ached.

Mrs. Surrel sat down stiffly in another armchair, filling it. She smiled at them, her mouth hard and thin beneath the lip-stick and her eyes glinting. She was letting them know that she was the boss right from the start. "Now," she said, "you came to talk about the elf problem?"

Miss Elmfield and Mr. Colly looked at each other to see who would speak first; then Mr. Colly coughed and said awkwardly, "Yes, that is correct. Your gardener, Mrs. Surrel, was speaking with me this afternoon, and he mentioned some trouble you've had with your monk—ah, erm—Chili-Pine."

"Oh yes." Mrs. Surrel nodded her head again, as Mr.

Colly took a quick sip of his coffee. "Mr. Runley *always* calls it a monkey-puzzle tree! Yes, it has been quite severely damaged. Mr. Runley thinks that it was 'blasted' by an elf. I must *admit* that at first I was incredulous. But after thinking about it for some time I find the idea of an elf not so improbable. Not half so unlikely as men landing on the moon."

"Exactly," agreed Mr. Colly. "We thought, Miss Elmfield and I, that you might be able to help us in capturing the elf and rescuing the children."

Mrs. Surrel put her cup and saucer on a little wobbly table. "Surely that is a very desperate plan, Mr. Colly?" she asked.

Miss Elmfield felt that she ought to join in. "We thought that since you know so much about magic and folk-lore, you could be of very great assistance to us."

"And you learnt about my interest in magic from Mr. Runley? Dear me, he is a very observant man." She put on a determined face. "You realise that if you set out to capture this creature you will not be dealing with something small or helpless."

Mr. Colly drew himself up tall in his chair. "We do know that it won't be particularly small—from the photograph."

"And," Mrs. Surrel said firmly, "if you say it is an elf then you must also admit that it has very real magical powers. Had you really thought of that? According to the folk-lore I've read, an elf has power over animals and plants—and, through magic, humans. Would you like some more coffee?"

"Yes please," Miss Elmfield said. "The last cup was

84

delicious." So Mr. Colly also mumbled that he would like some. Mrs. Surrel rose from her chair, stiffly upright all the way, and went into the kitchen again, having gathered up two of the cups. Miss Elmfield followed her with the third cup, leaving Mr. Colly to wonder miserably what Mrs. Surrel had done with her husband and son to keep them so quiet.

The ladies soon came back with the coffee. "Miss Elmfield and I were saying," Mrs. Surrel told Mr. Colly, "that when we start tracking down the elf, we shall need some form of protection. I suggest a rowan branch. Rowan has always been cited as a means of driving away witches and fairies."

"Yes," Mr. Colly muttered, "but what I want to know is. . . ."

"Where do we start searching for the creature?" Mrs. Surrel put in. "Precisely. I think myself that the forest is the clue to where he is. But, of course, if either of you has any other suggestions. . . ." She smiled, her eyes as hard as two penny-pieces, daring them to say anything.

They didn't say anything, and Mrs. Surrel, smiling more kindly, fetched some more biscuits.

Chapter 9

Next morning Mrs. Surrel's little blue mini was bouncing and hopping along the broken road, throwing the three people inside about until they felt like scrambled eggs. But Mr. Colly felt relieved. At least they were *doing* something, not just drinking coffee. They had a good idea of where the elf would be and they were going after him. Miss Elmfield wondered what they would say to the Headmaster when they got back to school, and then firmly put the idea out of her mind. Somehow she knew there was no time to spare, when you were dealing with an elf.

The road became impassable. Mrs. Surrel stopped the car, mudguard-deep in long grass, and they scrambled out, glad to ease their bruises and their cramped legs.

"It's going to be a long search," Miss Elmfield said, looking around at the ever-continuing trees. "How far did they say this goes on?"

"It covers the common, I think," Mr. Colly told her. "And probably more. I expect we shall just have to mill around until—until we trip over an elf or something."

Mrs. Surrel strutted around to the boot and unlocked it. The springy rowan branch imprisoned within coiled up in a mad attempt to escape, but got itself trapped as she raised the lid. Mrs. Surrel stepped aside to allow Mr. Colly to wrestle the branch free. She dusted her hands.

"I thought at first," she said, "that since the elf—er— erected the forest, the place to look for him would be in the middle of it. But we must be cunning. The elf will expect us to think that, I should say, from what I have read about elves, and so he will not be in the middle of the forest, but on the outskirts—or even right away from it."

"Oh, so we only have to search all the way around the forest—or the rest of the British Isles," Mr. Colly said. He had the rowan branch out of the boot now, holding it up as it quivered.

Mrs. Surrel drew herself up even straighter than she stood already. "Mr. Colly," she pronounced, "you have been urging us to pursue the creature. Now you complain about a little walking!"

Mr. Colly shrank back, his hair fairly parted by her words. After looking him up and down like a sergeant-major for a minute or two, Mrs. Surrel whisked around the car, locking the doors, and then led the way on the search.

They followed the edge of the forest for a long time, climbing over lumps of upturned concrete, fallen branches, huge tree roots, the women ripping their stockings on brambles, Mrs. Surrel losing her hat to overhanging tree limbs. The rowan that Mr. Colly carried kept getting caught up in the web of twigs and leaves above his head, and dragging him backwards off his feet. They were all thankful to stop for a rest, at a place where another road joined the ruined one they were following. Mr. Colly dropped his troublesome burden with a sigh, and mopped his face as he looked around. He saw, growing in the hedge, a bramble with bright, russet-red leaves. He crossed to it quickly to make sure that he had really seen it.

It was an Autumn bramble, in Spring. The women saw it too. And further along the undamaged lane was a tree whose leaves were turning yellow. After a short walk, Mr. Colly brought back a handful of burrs, and hazel-nuts. They studied these new mysteries in silence.

"He's altering the seasons," Mrs. Surrel said at last. "Really! Is nothing sacred?"

"It looks as if you were right," Mr. Colly had to admit. "It looks as if he's gone up this road, away from all those trees, doesn't it?"

Mrs. Surrel considered. Then she straightened her hat and pulled down her coat and dress. "Yes," she said, "I think it will do no harm to investigate this new road. If we find no further evidence of the elf, we can always come back." She marched off ahead once more, leaving Mr. Colly and Miss Elmfield to walk behind.

The elf had definitely been along this road. They saw blackberries, hips and haws, and wild sloe trees bearing ripe fruit. Above them rooks spun and scattered in confused flocks, and a fox scuttled low across the road in front of them.

They were approaching a small house, one whose garden had spilled out from the gate-posts on to the grass-verge. Daffodils, primroses, Christmas roses, sweet peas and tall white daisies all grew together, some with seed-heads and some without. On the gate leaned a man. He watched them coming down the road—a plump, stiff woman in high-heeled shoes, plastered with mud, a crumpled coat with matching hat, laddered stockings and runny make-up; a younger woman, equally untidy; and a man with leaves in his hair and a dirt-scrubbed suit, who was holding aloft a branch from a rowan tree. The man by the gate watched them as if he expected nothing but three such strange-looking people. As the trio came nearer to him, he said, "You'm after him then?"

There was no need to ask who 'he' was. "Yes," said Mrs. Surrel. The man nodded to himself. "I didn't believe he existed till this mornin', yer know. I couldn't explain all them trees, no, but I didn't believe in no fairies neither—till this mornin'."

"And then you saw what had happened to your flowers?" Miss Elmfield asked.

The man didn't answer with words, but swung open his gate, and waved them to follow him. He led them without a word to the back of the house, where two trees grew—one an apple, the other a pear. Both were weighed down with fruit. They all stared solemnly at the two trees.

"Didn't even have all their leaves last night," the man said calmly. He reached up, twisted a pear from its stalk, and bit into it. "Beautiful," he said. He picked a pear for each of them, and they wandered back to the gate. The pears *were* beautiful—ripe, juicy, soft.

Along the road the signs of the elf's presence increased. Autumn leaves, summer flowers, frosted gravel, dandelion 'parachutes' drifting by. A field of barley, half ripe and half green shoots; violets and holly berries in the same hedge.

They climbed up a bank and stood looking across the fields, the barley, the pasture, the dark green field with the hillock in the centre, fluffed over with trees. And as they stood there they heard the high, far-off notes of a whistle, which faded as the tune became lower. Mouths open, they listened until the snatch of music floated to them again, calling and laughing.

Mr. Colly jumped back down on to the road and looked along the hedge. "There's a gate here!" he called.

They cut straight across the barley field, instead of taking the long way around the hedges. It was hard going because they couldn't see where they were putting their feet—especially where the grain had ripened. But they didn't lose the sound of the whistle, though when they came to the hedge they had to fight and claw their way through, scratching faces, shredding stockings, and ripping coats.

But they could tell now exactly where the music was coming from—the hillock. Mr. Colly and Miss Elmfield were already running towards it, and with tuts of disapproval Mrs. Surrel forced herself to a trot, the highest speed she had moved at for some time.

She arrived at the bottom of the hill, red-faced, gasping, half in and half out of her shoes, clutching her hat, as the others started to climb. With squeaks of protest, horror and bad temper she bravely followed them, her feet slipping on the grass, her clothes catching on branches, her backside stuck up into the air as she went on to all fours. And then Mr. Colly jerked her up the last half-foot or so of the climb and they were all three of them facing the elf and his company.

In the centre of the trees on the hill was a small clearing, and in the clearing was a stone. Long and narrow, moss-covered, it rose from the ground at a slant; and at its foot leant the luchorpan, legs crossed, hat tilted back, looking at them in surprise. Near him sat the four children they were searching for, shoeless, jumperless, sockless, very dirty, and very happy. Miss Elmfield, watching them, thought that perhaps the luchorpan wasn't as black as he had been painted.

Mrs. Surrel took a deep breath and strutted to the front of her party. She sat her hat correctly on top of her head, pulled herself back into her coat and pushed her hair from her face. She said gaspingly, "So, we've caught you!"

The luchorpan just stared at her with wide, orange-flecked eyes. Mrs. Surrel found her own eyes held by that stare, and her mind too—for a frightening second she felt as if her mind was being sucked away. She blinked, shook her head, made herself look away from the elf's face altogether. She snatched the rowan branch from Mr. Colly and held it in front of her.

"Why did you have to come back and cause all this trouble?" she demanded.

The luchorpan stood up, took off his hat and held it to his chest. He blinked sleepily at the ladies and knuckled his eyes while he fought with a yawn. "I'm sorry, Me Lady, I am," he said. "I didn't mean it, I only woke up and things went from one to another. I didn't know what I was doin'."

Mrs. Surrel thought that these signs of repentance were all that could be wished for. She continued the treatment. "Your behaviour is disgraceful! Taking these children from their parents—disgraceful! And tampering with seasons, and the forest and the wolves, and that poor farmer! What *do* you think you're playing at?"

The luchorpan hung his head, clutching and folding the brim of his hat. He scuffed the ground with his bare toes. "I'm sorry, Me Lady, I swear by—b'me word of honour I am. But it's been such a long time an' all me tunes am mixed—did I want all them trees to lep up? I did not! 'Twas all a mistake. But—if yer'll only go away now, I'll sort it all out, sure I will. I will. Only—me music, it's dangerous for the human-kind like yerselves, and I wouldn't like to hurt yer."

The children behind him laughed as if he'd cracked a good joke. Mrs. Surrel began to have doubts about the elf's change of heart. She shook the rowan branch at him and cried, "Do you really think I believe you? Now let those children go at once! I'm tired of arguing to no good end!"

The luchorpan skipped back, away from the rowan leaves. There was a fish-flicker of anger in his eyes as he looked at Mrs Surrel. "Let them go?" he said indignantly. "Let them go? What way can I let them go when I'm not keepin' them?" He turned to the children behind him. "Come on then, the lady wants yer to go with her. Go on so. She'll treat yer fine, that's for sure."

The children got up and came forward, but it was the

luchorpan they were going to. Linda Windmore hung on his arm, swung on it, poked out her tongue at Mrs. Surrel, and said, "Don't want to go with you! See!"

"We're going to stay with him," Shirl said. "He's going to play us tunes."

Mrs. Surrel was shocked and worried. Who knew what harmful magic the elf had worked on the children? He was shamelessly using them to increase his own power. When he had no more use for them what would he do with them?

"I know all about you," she threatened. "Don't think I don't. You've been disturbing the seasons and tampering with time. If I were to get in touch with the Old One, you'd be in trouble, wouldn't you? *Wouldn't you, eh?*"

She was pleased to see the luchorpan jump. He was frightened. But he grinned suddenly, and nudged the children, who were as tall as he, and they grinned back. "What is it you know about the Old One?" the elf asked cockily. "Sure, and you are ignorant. And yer stand there an' tell me that yer goin' to the Old One yerself. Sun and moon, yer'll kill me laughin'!"

"Don't fool yourself!" Mrs. Surrel cried. "Don't fool yourself! I know all about your Old One. I know his name, don't I: I *can* get in touch with him, and he won't like what you're doing!"

And then Miss Elmfield said, "Who's the Old One?"

The luchorpan gave a wide and delighted grin. Miss Elmfield thought that she had never seen such a cunning and downright wickedness in a face before. The elf turned his grin on Mrs. Surrel and lifted the whistle to his mouth.

93

"Quickly, behind me, both of you!" Mrs. Surrel shouted, and her two companions scrambled into line behind her and the rowan branch.

The tune that came from the whistle was slow, slow and cold. It sank down inside you, crept through your whole body, cold like shadowed stone, and you felt stiff, stiff and mindless and blind. The music wrapped itself tight and clammily round everything, and not a sound was heard—anywhere. It was like the end of all things, the beginning of a silent, spinning eternity—and when it stopped . . . sound and life and light, touch and scent all rushed back in a crashing wave. It was like being born again.

But the rowan branch was dead.

Shrivelled, drooping and dead, it still hung from Mrs. Surrel's hand. But now it could give no protection. Mrs. Surrel, Miss Elmfield and Mr. Colly looked up to meet the luchorpan's evil grin and his sparkling brown eyes.

"Back!" Mrs. Surrel shouted, staggering on her high heels. "Run!" The other two were running before she opened her mouth. But it was of no use to try to outrun a tune. The first notes reached out for them, and Mrs. Surrel stopped and half-turned.

The music cascaded about her like snowflakes and windflowers, roses, light pearling on water and clever promises. It had a persuasion that stopped them all, but Mrs. Surrel suddenly stumbled towards the luchorpan, her arms held wide. "Darling!" she cried.

The luchorpan and the children laughed, and ran away down the opposite bank, through the trees. And

Mrs. Surrel blundered after them, shouting, "Lover! Honeybun! Come back, don't leave me!"

Mr. Colly tried to move, but his feet seemed to be buried in glue or thick mud. He could only thresh about, getting more and more angry, until he shouted, "Well, if he wants Mrs. Surrel with him, he has terrible taste in women, that's all I can say!"

"No." Miss Elmfield's voice came, very calm. "He took her because she's the only one who knows who the 'Old One' is. If I hadn't opened my big mouth he would never have guessed that only she knew! Now he has the children and Daphne!"

Mr. Colly stopped struggling like a bird in lime, and said comfortingly, "It wasn't your fault. You just didn't think . . . I mean. . . ."

"I ought to have thought!" Miss Elmfield said. She was quiet for a moment, and then said slowly, "The thing to do is to borrow some of those magic books of Daphne's and find out who—or what—this 'Old One' is. And contact it as Daphne said she'd do." She added thoughtfully, "If we ever got loose, of course."

Chapter 10

It didn't take long for the news of the wolf-infested, overnight forest to spread out of Halmsbury to the towns and cities around. Photographers from the big daily newspapers flocked about the place like rooks, and police marched stiff-legged in and out of the torn-up pieces of concrete, convinced that somebody was up to no good.

There were radio and television news programmes about the forest which had sprung up on Halmsbury Common between the hours of darkness and dawn, and the commentator would turn to a noted scientist, and ask him how it was that a forest of such size and age could grow in so short a time. The scientist would reply with a good many words which said nothing, because he didn't know any answer to the problem, any more than his questioner did.

There was just one being on earth who could have given the commentators and the scientists a true and full answer. But he had no intention of doing so. And if he had, they wouldn't have believed him.

He was a good distance from the forest now, across the fields, sitting with his company under an elm tree. Mrs.

Surrel, without her fine hat, her shoes, or her coat, sat beside him. The luchorpan, unable to sleep, was playing on his whistle to while away the time. The trickle of music lilted idly from one tune to another—'Ring-a-ring-a-roses', 'Three Blind Mice', 'Baa-baa-Black-Sheep'— all simply strings of sounds, which the luchorpan played without thought or effort. But when they were played on the green, black-banded whistle, the listeners saw the mice and the farmer's wife, the black sheep and the wool, and roses or plague-sores, according to their imaginations.

Once the music faded into a different kind of thing altogether, one of the pieces where the luchorpan hardly used his fingers at all, and the dumb notes he blew made living pictures for them. A picture of a girl's face, very dark hair, smiling mouth. The elf suddenly cut the tune off short, as he had done before, twisting the whistle into another, ordinary human tune.

"Who's that lady?" Shirl asked, and Lin listened for the answer.

"Aeve," said the luchorpan.

Shirl tried to fit this in with any kind of noise she had ever heard before. She couldn't. "What?"

"Aeve. It's of no good for you to try to say it. Yer could not, and yer'd only spoil the chirilt of it. She lives at the Howe—and that's where I come from. Sure, she's one of the biggest reasons I'm wantin' to get back." The luchorpan was quiet for a moment, then added, "The Howe's a place for yer—for me, anyway, not you. The human-kind don't live there long. The air and the music and the food and the drink—it's too much for 'em. Mind—the dead manage all right, they aren't human any longer, d'yer understand? Tobin's enjoyin' hisself there now, the big-mouthed gossoon, while I have to dance in circles over here."

"Why don't yer go back to this Howe then?" Lin asked.

"I will, I will," the luchorpan assured her, "when I've finished me business over here." And he started the music again, so that he wouldn't have to answer more questions.

Darkness came, hazy, softening the outlines of the trees and hedges. The night followed with a jump and they could hardly see each other. The luchorpan yawned, put away his whistle, got up and walked around the tree to ease the aches in his body.

"Come on," he said. "Let's not have any hanging about now! There's things that have got to be done, and then I shall be away off to the Howe. Come on, come on!" He pulled them to their feet and shook the sleep out of them. Then he waved to them to follow, and led them off across the fields again.

The elf made straight for Halmsbury, not trying to keep away from the roads and houses. He seemed to be walking to the rhythm of a tune, for he kept to the same brisk speed and never missed a step, never paused for even a second, no matter how he turned and twisted around bushes, trees, lamp-posts and other obstacles. Shirl asked him once or twice where they were going, but he had become silent and businesslike again and just ignored her.

They went right through the town and came at last

to a little church with a low wall around it, and short iron stumps sticking up to show where railings had once been before the scrapmen had come visiting. The notice board, above the ragged poster begging for money to support the roof, gave the church's name as 'Saint Michael's Parish Church'. But Mike said:

"Top Church! What we come here for?" It was known as Top Church for miles around, because it was considered to be at the top of Halmsbury town.

The luchorpan didn't answer Mike's question, but put one foot on the mossy wall and hopped over it on to the grass of the graveyard with a sigh of pleasure. The others followed him, unwilling, watching around them carefully, not liking to turn their backs on a small stone angel who stood over one of the graves. Top Church was such an unimpressive, shame-faced little building that it didn't even make them want to whisper as other churches did; but graveyards were another matter. They didn't believe in ghosts, of course . . . but they *were* frightened of them.

The luchorpan looked around at the graves, but didn't seem much interested in them. He stopped in front of the church's black doors to study the scrawled red writing and the five-pointed star painted on them in red. Chris came up beside him, and he nodded towards the writing with an inquiring look.

"It says 'Black Magic'," Chris told him. "That round the knocker ses 'Albion' an' 'Astle is King', and then that bit right down there at the bottom ses 'Jan loves Derry this is true'."

The luchorpan stood, soberly turning over in his mind

99

these new twists to the Christian religion. He shook his head, eyebrows raised. "They get dafter," he said, and began to walk round to the back of the church. The walls here were thick with spongy moss, and green trailing stuff, where for years the rain-water had spattered from the water-spouts along the roof; and the path was hidden by soupy green pools.

The back of the church was neglected, because most of the graves here were so old that there was nobody alive to look after them. The grass had grown long, tangled and wild, the trees thick and ragged. But the luchorpan seemed to like these graves better than those at the front of the church, and he parted the waist-high grass about them and trampled down the nettles, peering at the carved inscriptions. He caught the nearest person—Mike—by the shoulder, and pulled him to the grave, pointing to the writing. He put his finger-tips together, rubbed them, and a yellow flame appeared. By its light Mike read:

"Sarah Mahoney, laid to rest by her grieving husband in the year of Our Lord 1875, aged 35. May she rest in peace. Rene Mahoney, laid to rest by her mourning husband in the year of Our Lord, 1892, aged 40. May she sleep in peace . . . Josiah Woodall, died 1872, aged 58. Maria Woodall, beloved wife of above, died 1877, aged 62."

Mike and the luchorpan were absorbed in the little stories, but their companions began to feel the terrible weight of the cold, black quiet. They hung close to the elf, their eyes wide and strained, watching for something they didn't want to see, waiting with choked-off breath for the slightest movement, expected and dreaded.

100

"I don't like this," Lin whined, hating the thin sound of her voice, echoing in the black hole of night around them. "Let's go back."

"Whisht," said the luchorpan. "Whisht yer now, and listen."

"Died 1849, of the Cholera, Elias Thomas Armstrong, aged 30. He was a good man. Also died, in the same year, the wife of the above, Anne Armstrong, of the Cholera, aged 28. Also died, in the same year, their daughter Anne, aged 3, of the Cholera. God protect all innocents."

"Aah, it's lovely hearing," said the luchorpan. A low wind crept softly through the grass to rattle a branch on the church window. Shirl's hand jumped to her mouth, and she stood stock-still, listening.

"Died, of the Cholera, in the year 1849; Ronald Pitton, David Walsh, age 40, Grace and Patience Crossby, Mary Anne Luton, aged 12, Ethel Carter and Jechonias Carter. . . ."

"Aah, this is no good," the luchorpan said impatiently. "Come over here." He led the way into even longer grass, an even damper corner, even further from light. Rummaging through the grass, he found the hardness of a gravestone, and crumpled down the surrounding greenery with juicy noises.

"Read that one," he said.

Mike bent over, hands on knees. "Joseph—Joseph— I can't make out t'other name. Died 17—it's a six or an eight. Six I think—1761. That's old, ain't it?"

"It is," agreed the luchorpan. "They're gettin' older. Come over this way a little step. Now read this one—ah! Only the date."

Mike got down, scratched away lichen from the carving, peered closely. "1793."

"That's more like it!" said the luchorpan again, "Now read this one."

"Simon Weaver," Mike read, "Died 1808. An' this one's 1808. Obadiah Slater, di. . . ."

"O-ba-di-yah Slater!" cried the luchorpan. "O-ba-di-yah Slater! That's the man I want!"

"What are yer goin' to do?" Lin squeaked. There was a dreadful fear in her.

The elf had no time for her. "Will yer quiet now?" he demanded angrily. "It's not you that should be frightened. Now Mick, me hero, what does it say about O-ba-di-yah Slater?"

Mike began to read, thinking it a coincidence that the man should have the same name as himself. "Here lies the body of Obadiah Slater, who passed away from his grieving family in the year of Our Lord, 1808, at the age of 58. He was called to his place at the Lord's right hand—tch! That's a fine un, ain't it?"

"Oh, a fine one," said the luchorpan. "A fine one, O-ba-di-yah Slater."

"An'," Mike went on, "also the beloved wife of the above, Saranne Slater, who joined her husband in his rest, 1811, at the age of 59. They'm all beloved wives, ain't they? No hated wives."

"Aah—blessed!" said the luchorpan, not hearing him. "This is going to be tricky now. What did he have to have her put in with him as well for? I only want him."

"I don't suppose he had much say in the matter,"

102

Mike observed shrewdly. "He'd been under three year when they laid her to rest."

Lin came close to the luchorpan. She whispered, the words clogging with fear in her throat, "Are—are you goin' to bring him out?"

"Eh?" said the luchorpan, shaken from his thoughts. "Bring him out?"

"Are you goin' to bring him out of the grave?" Lin croaked.

The luchorpan looked up at her from the grass, his face full of disgust and exasperation. He threw off his hat in temper. "He's not much use *in* the grave, is he?" he cried, amazed at her stupidity. "Only a heap of old bones *in* the grave!"

Lin made a little whimpering sound. Shirl said, "That's what we *mean*."

The luchorpan didn't understand. He stared at their worried faces, white against the dark and the hunched black yew trees. He shouted, "What for are yer frightened at all? He'll only be a man." He looked at the grave and added, with wicked pleasure, "A dead old man."

Shirl was gripping Lin's arm. She asked, "But—but won't he look 'orrible?"

The luchorpan nodded. " 'Orrible. Oh he will indeed. He couldn't help but look 'orrible, that O-ba-di-yah Slater."

Lin gasped and began to cry. Shirl stared at the grave without moving, not even blinking, hardly breathing. The luchorpan took the whistle from his pocket, scowled at them, sat down in front of the gravestone. Shirl closed her eyes tightly.

103

The music burst out into the night in a gleaming flood that took tiredness, cold and fear with it into the air and away. The notes danced, their fingers and feet couldn't help but tap, and their heads nod. The music sailed up and up and up above them, hovered, swooped joyfully.

Chris began to feel that there was someone else with them—the gravestone seemed to have grown taller. He peered closer and gulped. Lin squealed.

In front of them, shadowy, dim, stood a man much taller than the luchorpan, taller than Mrs. Surrel, his shoulders and chest much broader. He was stooped, his arms hung loose and bone-thin, his legs sagged at the knees. His head stuck forward on a long, skinny neck. His eyes seemed like dark holes.

The five humans stared horror-stricken at the ghost, while the music of the tin-whistle tumbled about them. And under the shaping of the pipe's sound the figure by the gravestone became more solid, clearer. They felt their muscles go weak as they relaxed with relief.

It was only a man. A man with a tired, kind, quiet face. He was dressed in a very similar fashion to the luchorpan—dirty, crumpled corduroy trousers, baggy grey work-shirt—but he wore no hat. Lin, watching him, almost loving him—she was so relieved that he seemed normal—thought he looked like Mike.

The tall ghost-man peered about him, blinked, raised his head on his lanky neck and sniffed at the cold, damp air with a large blunt nose. He looked down at the luchorpan, who was still allowing single notes to drop

104

from the whistle's mouth. He said slowly, "Awright. I know yer. What doest want?"

The luchorpan laid the whistle down and tilted his head back to see the ghost. He smiled lazily as he thought about what to say. The ghost was so much bigger than the elf that Mike wondered whether he might not be more powerful. Finally the elf said, "Now what d'yer think, O-ba-di-yah Slater?"

Obadiah shook his heavy, grey head. "I got no ideas, but whatever it is, I know it be no good. There worn't never no good come outa you." His voice was thick, deep, slow, heavy as his bones.

The luchorpan grinned suddenly, and the ghost shivered. Chris felt sorry for him, because he could feel Obadiah's fear. Mike was trying to think where he had seen the ghost before. The luchorpan asked, "D'yer remember Tobin McGraw, O-ba-di-yah Slater?"

The ghost shook his head and his whole body quivered. "I don't think—as I've 'eered the name," he said cautiously.

The luchorpan tapped his finger on the ground, and whistled to himself between his lips. Chris felt that everything was happening much too slowly, and that if they didn't stop talking and tapping and whistling, his mind would snap into pieces. The elf said thoughtfully, "Yer have never heard the name. There's a thing. But yer should know the man, O-ba-di-yah Slater—yer killed him."

The ghost trembled and dragged a hand down his face. "That was a long time ago," he said, his voice burring low. "A long time. I ain't forgot. I didn't know the name."

"But yer killed the man. What matter how long ago? Yer killed the man. Here's yerself, O-ba-di-yah Slater, lived to be an *old* man, with a beloved wife, and how many children?—*How many children, I asked yer, O-ba-di-yah Slater?*"

"Eleven," Obadiah said. "Four daughters and seven sons."

"Eleven! Eleven babies. Four beautiful daughters to see yer comfortable when yer got to be an *old* man, and seven sons big as yerself for pride. And you not even knowin' the name of the man yer killed when he'd hardly finished twenty years. And he never had any of those good things."

The ghost shook his head again. "I didn't mean to kill him. I was drunk an' evil an' scared. 'E was jead afore I knowed—Hell! I didn't know I *could* kill a man. I didn't know I was that strong. I didn't mean it."

"There's comfort," crooned the elf. "O-ba-di-yah Slater didn't mean to kill yer, Tobin. He swears so himself. Does that mean he was never killed at all? But he was dead when I fetched him."

The ghost spread big, thick-skinned hands and cried, "I killed him! I did it! I say it 'ere for yer. I've bin sorry for it all me life, but——" he shouted at the elf—"but I say this as well: I'm glad I was neverof ol enough to confess! I'm glad I've had my life! Killin' him was accident, I didn't hit him meanin' to kill him, 'twas accident—an'—an'—would hangin' me have brought him back? Eh? No, it wouldn't. An'—an'—I'd like to know what yer've come for 'cos yer can't touch me now!"

The luchorpan just smiled.

"Yer can't!" Obadiah shouted even louder.

The luchorpan ducked his head, and when he looked up again his expression was completely different. He grinned, very friendly, and jerked a thumb at Mike over his shoulder. "Tell me now, did yer ever see that one before?"

Obadiah's eyes jerked wildly up to Mike's face, flicked away again to the elf, then jumped back. He gazed at Mike for a long, long time with blank, dead eyes that seemed covered with a skin of milk. Then he smiled, tired and kind. "Ar," he said, gentler, calmer, a cat-warm purr creeping into his voice. "Ar. I ain't ever seen him meself afore, but I know him for who he is. Me Gran'son. Or one on 'em."

The luchorpan nodded. "Great, Great, Great, Great, Great, Great Gran'son." He stopped to let this information sink in. Obadiah stole a look at Mike again, smiled again, held out his big, square shovel of a hand. "I'll just shake th'ond, lad. I'm a lucky man, bain't I, seein' me own Great, Great, Great, whatever it was Gran'son. D'yer know, tha look the spit o' me."

Mike, driven by hammered-in politeness, put out his own hand, and Obadiah's folded over it, two or three times, it seemed. But instead of being hot, like the hands of most big men, the hand was cold, with a cold that reached into Mike's body to suck out his bones. Obadiah saw the fright in the boy's face, and let him go.

"Sorry, lad, I forgot," he said in his deep voice. He suddenly looked from Mike to the elf and back again, anger flickering up in him. "What tha doin' with him? Get on home, goo on! I'm tellin' thee. Tek tha friends

107

wi' thee. Tha don't want to goo with him, he ain't human-like."

The luchorpan turned his grin on Mike, and Mike stepped back from Obadiah. "You're dead," he said. "You're nothin' to do wi' me. You can't tell me what to do."

Obadiah stared at him for a moment, and then turned back to the luchorpan, his shoulders sagging.

"Don't look like that, O-ba-di-yah," said the elf, in his new, friendly tone. "Listen to me now—I'm not one to bear a grudge, as a rule, yer know that. You killed the best man o' the human-kind I ever knew—but Old One! he would have died anyway. The thing—the thing that used to hurt most was me having to get him to the Howe, and then I had to stay behind. Sure, yer can't go forever without proper rest and it's hard work moving a grown man. I had to stay all this time away from me own people—tragic it is. But after two hundred years, I'm tellin' yer, O-ba-di-yah, that doesn't matter so much either. Forgive and forget, that's what I think. But—" the elf held up a finger dramatically—"but, I thinks to meself, anybody can make words. So I'll prove that I've got no hard feeling against yer. I'll take yer for a walk." Obadiah's mouth fell open, and the luchorpan hurried on before the ghost could speak. "In the sun, O-ba-di-yah, warm sun an' rain, d'yer remember rain, how bright it is an' how it makes things grow? There'll be cornfields an' apples, an' the canal, an' flowers if yer like that sort o' thing, an' birds a-bawlin' their heads off. Wouldn't yer like that, Obadiah—all in the sun, wouldn't yer?"

The figure of Obadiah shook, quivered, in the dark cold. Now there, now not. "Don't," his deep voice said. "Don't say things like that, for God's sake. I can't leave me grave, what's dead's dead. Goo away, goo on, leave me in peace."

The luchorpan blew lightly on the whistle, blew a lemon-yellow day and a shower of rain; flowers, birds, just as he had described. The ghost put a hand to his head.

"Oh yer a devil an' no mistake," he said. "The dead are dead. They're dead 'cos that's how they should be. Them as goes walkin' only makes theirselves miserable. They're lonely an' things have changed for 'em—this churchyard's changed! I'm here, safe, with Anne—you just leave us. . . ."

The whistle sang itself through the seasons. Spring, Summer, Autumn, Winter: the seasons of two hundred years ago when Obadiah was young.

"Shut up! Shut yer mouth!" Obadiah cried. "Goo 'way an' leave me alone. I ain't gooin' to be fool enough to go with yer. Just goo away!"

The whistle, for answer, swung into a complicated dance tune, a jig tune. The notes wove themselves in and out, up, down, round about, to such a patternless pattern that the head spun to listen to it. It promised—happier things.

"Life's only good once!" Obadiah cried out against the tune. "Only once! Tha can't come back an' be happy again. Once tha'm dead, tha'm dead, an' the grave's the place for thee. I just want to lie down again, leave me alone! Please, for God's sake—can't yer *see* that?"

The luchorpan stopped the tune and said mournfully, "Obadiah, I want to show yer that I don't hate yer any more, I want to show that I'm—I'm changin' with age, an' I forgive yer. I'll tell yer what I'll do—I'll give yer your own time. I'll give yer yer life again, Obadiah. . . .!"

"Hey now. . . ." Obadiah began warningly.

The luchorpan never noticed his interruption. ". . . Sunshine over the fields, and the cart-horses on Mayday, d'yer remember? The brasses on the horses an' the time yer got the first baby from yer wife, d'yer remember, Obadiah Slater? What that baby looked like, an' what yer thought, an' what yer said, an' what she said, d'yer remember?"

"I do!" Obadiah said fiercely. "I do! Leave me alone. Just leave me alone."

"Sure yer remember," went on the luchorpan. "But how much do yer remember? Yer'll have forgot a lot an' that's a terrible shame, an' I could be showin' it to yer again. Sunshine now. Yer don't remember sunshine now, do yer?"

He played a few notes that were pure sunshine and got to his feet, coming to below Obadiah's shoulder. He looked into the farmhand's face, then touched his hat. "Aah well, I can see yer want nothing to do with it. I'll be away." He began to walk through the long, damp graveyard grass, to the corner of the church. The others followed him, fading with the darkness, and the place became more silent, more lifeless. Only Mike turned to squint through the wet, foggy dusk at the solitary figure by the gravestone.

110

"Wait!" Obadiah cried out with such terror and loudness that Chris's heart leapt up and rattled against his ribs. The luchorpan stopped, turned, and waited.

"What about me?" Obadiah gasped.

The luchorpan only waited.

"You just gooin' to leave?" the ghost shouted, and the echo from the wet church wall jeered at him, again and again, until the cold breeze drowned it out.

"Yer don't want me about yer, O-ba-di-yah Slater," the elf said.

"I can't get back to the grave," Obadiah pleaded. "I can't get back."

"Then don't," said the elf. "Walk. Up and down. Down and up. There's plenty of room and it won't be too hard on an old man." He played one last phrase on his whistle, a snatch of music that was the story of all the good times in Obadiah Slater's life. "It's a shame yer don't want to come, O-ba-di-yah Slater," said the luchorpan. "Yer'd have been back before yer was missed."

And he led on again, around the corner of the church.

Obadiah stood and shivered in the dark. He was cut off from his own place in his grave, helpless, stranded in an unknown world. But around the corner was something as inhuman as he was. The only one who could give him back the grave's peace. He tipped forward, trying to move, but the stiffness of death held him. Slowly, creaking, he forced himself along, but with each of his painful steps he thought of the quick and easy moving of the luchorpan. He would lose it . . . he would

111

lose it . . . step by slow, agonising, maddening step he fought his way to the church, around the corner, along the wall, around the second corner. . . . The luchorpan was waiting for him, standing by the low church wall, leaning one shoulder on a white stone angel.

Chapter 11

Miss Elmfield and Mr. Colly sat in Miss Jenns's living-room, with Mrs. Surrel's books about them. It was three in the morning and they had been reading since two o'clock of the afternoon before. The luchorpan's spell had worn off at last, but by then he and his company were far away, and there was nothing they could do for Mrs. Surrel but go home and study the books she had lent them the evening before. Mr. Colly raised his throbbing eyeballs from the narrow lines of words to the blurred picture of floppy-eared cocker spaniels on the wall, and groaned aloud.

But the time had not been wasted. They had found out who the Old One was. There were scribbled notes about him on the paper which lay thick around Miss Elmfield's feet. The notes gave warnings, descriptions, spells—all copied from the books. Mr. Colly reached out and picked up one of the sheets.

'He was an honest, elderly man, grey-bearded, and dressed in the old fashion, a pair of grey breeches gartered about the knee, a black bonnet on his head'.

Mr. Colly shook his head—gently—as he read it. The woman who had, centuries before, spoken those words had supposedly been a witch, and should have known what she was talking about. But Mr. Colly's mind couldn't think of the Old One like that. Not now that he knew who he was.

Another little scrawl said: 'He appeared in the form of a black ram'. Mr. Colly almost smiled. Not for the life of him could he imagine the luchorpan speaking so respectfully of a sheep.

'A mickle black, rough man, bearing on his head the horns of a ram.' That was more like it. Mr. Colly turned it over in his mind. 'Rough' would mean shaggy, or hairy. 'Mickle' meant 'big'. Big, black and shaggy with ram's horns.

On the other side of the paper was a list of names that Miss Elmfield had put down. They were all names that the Old One had been called by at some time, or in some country. The Old One, the Evil One, the Foul Fiend. Hern, King Herna, Himself, and Old Nick. The Master, The Black One, Old Gentleman, Old Scrat, Cluftie, Clootie, Cloutie and Boucca. Mr. Colly came to the last name and stopped. He said, "Wonderful, isn't it? We've got to go and have a nice friendly chat with the Devil himself."

The big horse skittered round and the young man followed it, hissing and whistling through his teeth. He had ribbons hanging from his hand, stirring softly across his thick wrist in the wind, and bright horse-brasses, crescents, horse-shoes, stars and trefoils dangled from his arm. He patted the horse's shoulder, that was level with his head, soothing and calming, and then moved back to its tail, plaiting the ribbons into its rough hair. Obadiah laughed, "A beautiful horse, the General," he said. "Beautiful."

But with the guiding of the whistle the horse and man slipped away, changed to laughter, then to the same young man sitting on a big, wooden kitchen chair, with a baby on his knee, a baby that grinned and tried to pull itself upright by tugging on the hairs that grew out between the open flaps of the man's shirt-front. And the man roared out and shouted, "Murder!" to someone they couldn't see, but they heard a woman's absent-minded laugh, warm and low as bubbling stew in a pot.

Things changed again, changed to the same man walking across a frosty, ploughed field, in the tingling cold, yet with his shirt-sleeves rolled up, and mopping at his face. They could see him stumble a little as the hardened plough ridges refused to crumble but turned his feet under him; and they saw the feathered blast of mist from his mouth as he shouted when a pheasant flew up from the hedge. But the whistle clouded the picture away, and all they could remember of it were black elms against a clear grey-blue sky.

The whistle's music sounded then like the screaming of pigs, and the rumbling of a kettle, the screeching crack of new ice, the clank of a spoon against the side of an almost emptied bowl—all the good sounds in life, though they might not be what the poets talk about—and the ghost of Obadiah Slater stood straighter, with its chest stuck out, and the wrinkles around its mouth and eyes were stronger.

The music died away and they were sitting by a hole, under the hawthorn hedge, near the place where the luchorpan had first met the children.

Obadiah shook his head, and his thin mouth lifted slightly at the corners. He blinked. "Like livin' again," he said. "Just like livin' again." He shook his big, blunted head some more, lifted one big-knuckled hand, fingers spread, let it fall helplessly. "Wish my Anne was here to see it."

"She was," said the luchorpan. "That was yerself. Yer were in two places at once. That was herself. She was too."

Obadiah nodded. "Ar," he said. "But I'm here, an' her's back there. Least I know her's safe." He was quiet for a while and then hissed through his teeth, as a horse groom does when the dust is rising from a horse's coat. "It's a good thing to be young an' alive," he said, "when tha can pick anvil up an' feel tha back pullin' wi' weight on it, an' not have to worry about hurtin' thyself an' what the wife an' kids'd do if tha was crippled. Shh-shh-shh—it's a thing tha don't appreciate when thee've got it—it's on'ny when tha finds tha can't lift like tha could, an' tha can't run for longer than it takes to lie wi'out stoppin' for a breath. Tha wish thee was young again then, right enough! When the wages goo down 'cos thee can't work like thee could, oh tha don't half wish tha was young again!—but it ain't possible, not then. . . ." His voice tailed off.

"Aye," the luchorpan whispered in sympathy. "'Tis not possible—till the apples grow on an ivy tree." He cocked an eye at the man. "Would yer think that impossible, O-ba-di-yah Slater?"

116

Obadiah returned his look, his eyes crinkling into brown wrinkles, though his mouth did not smile. "Noaw," he said. "Naow. I shouldn't like to live again. Not me whole life, noaw. There's things in me life as I shouldn't like to goo through again—not for nobody. An' then, when thee'm old an' no use t'anybody, it ain't so bad to die. Then the grave's *yower* place, an' tha'm happy theer. Happy like sleeping. . . . Noaw, I shouldn't like to live again."

Chris leaned into the conversation, asking quickly, while he had the opportunity, "Do you—elves an' that like—do you die?"

The elf looked at him coolly for a moment, and then replied, "To them that asks no questions, is told no lies."

"True enough," said Obadiah. "True enough."

He and the luchorpan were talking like old friends, Shirl thought, but then she saw the elf turn his face away from Obadiah and lift up his hand to hide behind while he smiled. It wasn't a pleasant smile. It was the smile of a person—or thing—that is winning.

"Well," said the luchorpan, pulling at the hawthorn leaves above his head, "I'll give yer two lives then, O-ba-di-yah Slater. I'll show yer what the country's like now. It's not so bad at all, the human-kind haven't changed it much. Would yer like that, would yer?"

Obadiah hissed again, through his teeth, thoughtfully, and threw a stone into the green canal. Then he grinned at the luchorpan, his red and brown face folding into many lines around his eyes and mouth, a line of white teeth showing between his lips. "Ar, ar, I would that, ad! Take tha chances while they're theer, I reckon. 'Tain't every mon as gets the chance to see the future, is't?"

The luchorpan shook his head with a smile.

"Ar," Obadiah breathed, "I'd like to see what they done wi' place."

The luchorpan grinned as if Obadiah was the friend he loved most. He put his hand out to Mrs. Surrel. "Come on, me darlin'." And Mrs. Surrel twittered with delight, because the luchorpan was going to let her sit by him; and him half a head shorter than her.

The luchorpan lifted his whistle.

"He's the Devil all right," Miss Elmfield yawned. "But the question is—how do we get into touch with him? I've read dozens of spells and chants, and goodness knows what, but I've not found anything that sounds as if it might *work*."

"I've not found anything that sounds as if it might *not* work, even," Mr. Colly said, shutting another book, and resting his forehead on his hand. "These books I'm reading have a lot to say about the Devil, but they're very careful to skate around anything telling you how to reach him."

There was only the rustle of turned pages for a while and then Mr. Colly burst out, "I don't know that I *want* to reach him, not even for the children and Mrs. Surrel. Big hairy black thing—too dangerous by half for me!"

"Big hairy black thing? Oh no—" Miss Elmfield looked

118

up from the book. "No, that's too childish. No, he'll be an old man with a long beard—why would he be called the Old One, if he wasn't?"

She went on reading, and Mr. Colly went on reading and yawning. Suddenly he said, "What about giving up for now? We can't work around the clock like this."

Miss Elmfield continued to read until she had reached the bottom of the page. Then she looked up, blinking bleary eyes. "You go home if you want to," she said. "But I don't think I could sleep if I went to bed. This is important. And I think we *must* find out how to contact the Devil *soon* because it's obvious that we can't do anything against the elf ourselves, and who knows but that the thing might decide he doesn't want his company any more."

"Oh God," Mr. Colly said, "you're right." He picked up a book, a sheet of paper and a pencil, ready to work. Then he cast them aside again to say, "I don't know that I'm inclined to trust someone who has a reputation like the Devil."

Miss Elmfield retorted, "Daphne said that the Old One would help, and she ought to know."

They saw the canal, not as it lay sullen, dirty, oil-besmeared between factory walls, but as it ran across country, beneath little stone bridges, with daffodils growing on the banks.

They explored woods, woods that were still wild and free-growing, not the stiff, uniformed ranks of the Forestry Commission.

They sailed over mountains, not mountains that had been hacked away as men searched for coal, iron-ore, limestone or road space; but Welsh mountains, lonely, misty, a kestrel hovering overhead.

They saw moors, those moors that had no gravelled roads crossing them, no clashingly coloured, dirty 'caffs'; but moors of brown and blue and emerald green, black pools, cutting winds and wandering sheep.

They sat in a moorland valley, on the tussocky grass, watching a dragon-fly jumping above a stream. The luchorpan said, "They haven't changed it much, have they now, O-ba-di-yah? It wouldn't be hard to live here, would it?"

Obadiah sighed. "It's better 'an it was," he said. "All the open space."

"Look at that sheep," Lin said, "the little black one comin' down there." They looked to where she pointed and saw the lamb trotting down a steep sheep-path through the heather and fern, bleating and bleating.

"Poor little beggar's lost his Mam," Obadiah said, and laughed. "Her'll come for him, an' her'll say, 'Wheer dost think thee've bin all this time? I'll have top layer o' skin of thee!' I allus did think it good the way t'ewes could allus find little uns, no matter how far off they got."

He leaned backwards on one elbow and began to crumble a curled fern into tiny bits that stuck to his fingers, smelling strong and sweet. He sighed again, filled with grass scent and cold air, joy and sadness.

"Now," the luchorpan said, "back to the grave."

Obadiah sat bolt upright, and gawped at him. Then

his head sank, showing the back of his lean, brown neck, with the grey hair curling about it. "I forgot that," he said, his voice rough. "I was believin' meself alive again."

The children, watching and listening, felt cold, as if the walls of the grave were closing about them too, cutting out the light. The straining bleat of a sheep seemed the saddest thing in the world. Obadiah sighed again, raised his head, and grinned. "It's daft, ain't it?" he said. "I can feel me bones achin' a'ready—an' I ain't got no bones! I'd be better in grave, no troubles theer." But the grin stayed a little sick on his face.

The luchorpan spoke with lowered head to hide a smile. But his voice was sorry. "I don't like to send yer back, but I have to, I see. I'd like to see yer about again, I would sure—but I can't. I see that now. It would be disturbin' the order of things an' it would bring trouble down about us like tons and tons of bricks. D'yer understand, Obadiah? D'yer see it's not me feelin' evil?"

"Oh ar," Obadiah said listlessly. "Ar. 'Tain't thee, it's the laws. There's allus summat. Not as I'd like to stop for a long time, mind—it's too tirin'. But just a bit longer'd be good."

The luchorpan sighed now as if his heart ached. He lifted his whistle and blew one sharp note that stung their ears; and then they were back under the hawthorn hedge with a slam and a jerk, and a swinging feeling in their stomachs. The children's bodies felt very tired and weak. They flopped about like rags in the wind.

They looked around at the scene—the green and dirty canal, the few grubby houses with the flying pink washing, the battered old black lock gates, locked stiff from

121

disuse; the lacy hawthorn leaves above their heads, the cold sky showing through. They stared at these things as if they had last seen them from a very long distance away, a very long time ago. It was strange, the mind needed time to get used to it.

At last the flicker and flounce of a pink sheet roused Obadiah. He stirred in the long grass, groaned, and said, "Let's be gooin' then."

The luchorpan didn't move. Neither did anybody else. The luchorpan was hunched around his own knees, examining his own clasped hands which were held in front of him, the whistle sticking up from them. He murmured:

"Obadiah. Listen now. I have something to say to you. . . ."

"What is dead is dead," said the luchorpan. "Sure yer've said that yerself, Obadiah. If I give a dead thing life, that's disturbin' the order o' things, an' upsettin' the balance. Is that not right, Obadiah?"

"Well—I don't know," Obadiah said suspiciously. "It sounds awright to me."

"It is right. But—but if yer give a death for a life or—or—if yer remove somethin' from life in exchange for the life given—then the balance is there again, an' everything's fine. That's also right, Obadiah Slater."

There was an uneasy silence on the tow-path, except for the 'wop!' of a sheet slapped out sharply by the wind.

"Just what are you workin' round to?" Obadiah asked slowly, his head turned to one side.

The luchorpan stared out over the canal before answering. He was combing Obadiah's mind, watching how the ghost would feel about the various things he could say before he said them. He decided that direct attack was best.

"If I remove someone from life in exchange for your life, you could live again, Obadiah."

Obadiah was dumb for a second, then laughed loudly, as the luchorpan had known he would. "Who'd die just so's I could live?" he asked. "Saftness! I've told thee as I shouldn't like to live again."

"Yer wouldn't have to live yer whole life again," the elf said. He moved this argument in as you might move in a counter in a game of draughts, to stop one of your men being taken off. "But yer said yer'd like a bit longer here. I can only give yer that by givin' yer life. For a time."

"I don't know," said Obadiah, serious again, and very cautious.

"Mick'd die for yer," the luchorpan said smoothly, "Mick would. He's yer gran'son, isn't he?"

Obadiah pointed a threatening finger at the elf. "Here now," he said, angry. "As if I'd ask a child to give up any of his life, even a few minutes! I'm tired now, an' I'll be glad to get back if you'll kindly oblige."

But the luchorpan had turned his full attention on Mike. He stared straight into the boy's eyes, and Mike couldn't look away, even though he wanted to. And he wanted to, because the elf's eyes were changing, getting larger until they were the only things to be seen: misting over, becoming transparent—it was frightening.

"Yer would, wouldn't yer, Mick, Mick, wouldn't yer? Oh, yer a fine lad, a lad a Gran'father could be proud of. Brave, brave lad. It would be nothin', this goin' away, it'd not hurt—and think. Yer'd never be cold again, or hungry, or miserable, or disappointed, or scared, or in pain. . . ." The words echoed softly, like drum-rolls or waves, or clapping. . . . There was another voice, very far away, very weak, which called, "Or happy, Mike, or warm, or surprised, or loved! Don't listen to him! Don't listen! Oh, for Christ's sake, don't listen!"

The luchorpan's words purred right on over the voice. "All yer'll ever get out of life, Mick, is disappointment, sickness and misery. That's a true thing. The strange thing about happiness is that it dies in a second, but misery and shame, they last for ever . . . and ever. Everybody'd be better dead, Mick . . . or never born . . . that's a true thing."

And a music came silently up inside Mike, and the luchorpan's eyes were windows to look through and see the things the music spoke of . . . good things . . . secret things . . . things horrible and beautiful because they could not be understood and there was nothing to compare them with.

Obadiah shouted, he tried, he shouted until he was empty of spirit and breath, but he couldn't move from where he sat, and Mike couldn't hear him any more. And then Mike vanished. Like a pricked bubble. It wasn't possible and their minds swayed away from the fact, and struggled to disbelieve.

"He's gone!" Shirl said at last.

124

"I'm sure it's all for the best if Toolie thought it all right," Mrs. Surrel said.

The luchorpan had not stopped playing, but only switched to an ordinary tune, a heavy, dull tune. It was played at Obadiah, and the man—he was no ghost now—found his eyes bleary, his body paralysed, as he fought to get up and break the elf, his neck wobbly and weak under his head. He flopped and slumped sideways. The luchorpan stopped playing and kicked the sleeper with his foot. "Sleep well, old man," he said. "I hope yer enjoy yerself when yer wake up."

"Where's Mike?" wailed Lin.

Chapter 12

Mr. Colly knew he was awake because he felt as if his head had split into many separate parts, and every part was throbbing like a miniature heart. He opened his eyes, and immediately screwed them shut again as light blazed and burnt against his eyeballs. Then a voice said, "I've made you some coffee. Do you want it?"

He moved his hand in front of his eyes and risked opening them again—not very wide. He recognised Miss Elmfield, and wondered what on earth she was doing in his house.

"Do you want the coffee?"

He saw that he was on Miss Jenns's settee, in her living-room, and not in his bed at home. And he saw why he had been so uncomfortable. He had been sitting on the settee, and he must have fallen asleep, and just toppled over.

He drained his cup, and memories of the day before seeped into his mind. "What about the Devil?"

"Oh yes," Miss Elmfield said. "On the table—I've written out the Lord's Prayer. Backwards."

Miss Jenns came in with a cup of coffee. "I thought I'd take the dogs and my camera up to Devilstun and ask if I could take some photographs of the stone. I was reading in—oh, in some local newspaper or another, the other day, about it. It's supposed to be very old—the stone, I mean, not the newspaper, and if the farmer let the newspaper man go to see the stone I don't see why he shouldn't let me, do you, dear? The stone's in his fields, you see."

"No, Auntie," Miss Elmfield said, "I don't see why he shouldn't." She heaved herself up and began to arrange the straight-backed chairs in a circle against the coffee table.

"What *are* you doing?" her aunt wanted to know.

Miss Elmfield thought before answering. She didn't want to alarm the old lady. So she smiled and said, "We're setting a trap for that leprechaun you photographed, Auntie."

Miss Jenns tittered. "Really? *Do* call me if you catch him!" She finished her coffee, and went out as her niece completed the circle of chairs.

"There you are! Read your piece," Miss Elmfield said. "And come inside the circle. All the best spells have circles in them."

Mr. Colly obeyed, pushing a chair aside, and replacing it after him. "Do I just read it now?"

"Might as well," Miss Elmfield said, trying to sound as if she didn't care much.

Mr. Colly took another long breath and began, stumbling over the complicated sounds: "Nema, reve d-na reve rof y-rolg, e-h-t d-na rewop——" he stopped for breath and looked uncertainly at Miss Elmfield, who nodded. "Sessapsert. Ru-o su evigrof daerb y-liad——"

127

They were getting too near the ending for his liking. He had to stop to clear his throat of the fear that clogged it and wipe his wet hands down his jacket. "-Y-h-t, emoc modgink y-h-t, eman y-h-t eb dewollah, nevaeh ni tra o-h-w re-h-taf ru-o."

And that was the ending. Mr. Colly licked his lips and held his breath; Miss Elmfield waited with clasped hands, her head spinning with fear.

But the only thing that came in was the dog Candy, pushing open the door and yapping. They looked nervously round the room, but there was nothing that could be taken for a devil or the Devil. Miss Elmfield sighed, but she didn't know whether it was with disappointment or relief.

"Perhaps we did it wrong," Mr. Colly suggested. He was very relieved and knew it. "You wrote the words back to front as well as backwards. Perhaps they should only have been backwards."

"We'll try it!" Miss Elmfield snatched the paper and a pencil.

"What? Now? Already?"

But Miss Elmfield was scribbling away. He watched her doubtfully, feeling sure that he would be the one who had to read it again. He was.

They got nothing from the second recitation but a fresh fright. "I don't think this Lord's Prayer bit works," Mr. Colly said. "So what do we do now?"

Miss Elmfield surprised him by suddenly shouting: "Satan! Devil! Beelzebub! Lucifer! Old One! Old Gentleman! Hern!"

"What was *that* in aid of?" he demanded.

128

"Oh, I remembered reading somewhere that if you repeated the Devil's name aloud he would appear. Only he's got so many names I didn't know which one to say," Miss Elmfield explained breathlessly.

" 'Say', not 'shout'," Mr. Colly reproached her.

"Well, that doesn't seem to work either." She looked at the books that were piled about. "Those books said that the Devil was the same as the old god—the old hunter god—and he's connected with the earth and the seasons. So if you took earth and water—and salt, because that's very important, isn't it?—and burned it? For fire. Because those are the elements, you know—fire, air, earth and water."

Mr. Colly shook his head. "I'm beginning to think it's all a mistake anyway, and there is no Devil. Or if there is, there's no way of reaching him."

Just then Miss Jenns came in again, looking under cushions for leads.

"Miss Jenns," Mr. Colly suddenly asked, "where did you say you were going?"

"Devilstun, dear. To see . . ."

"Devilstun! Devil's stone that should be, I'll bet. Going over Devilstun way, they say, it's quicker by Devilstun way. But it's said fast, so you don't think—Rosalyn, that's the place to bury your salt and stuff!"

Both ladies stared at him.

"Devil's stone," he explained more slowly. "It's an old stone monument, is it? It'll be a pagan place of worship. If it's the old gods you're after now, that'll be the place to start from. Won't it?"

Miss Elmfield jumped up and ran into the kitchen. "Some salt from the pantry!" she said. "Somebody find some matches. Tap water will have to do, in case there isn't a stream. I'll take it in a bottle."

"Are you coming with us?" asked the bewildered Miss Jenns.

"Yes, Auntie," Miss Elmfield called from the kitchen. "To catch a leprechaun."

"Ooh!" said Miss Jenns.

The bus stopped just by the 'Green Man', and Miss Jenns with her dogs Candy and Sweetie, Miss Elmfield, with a bag of salt, and Mr. Colly with a bottle of water, got off.

"Now let me think," Miss Jenns said, as the bus grunted and grumbled away. "If I remember rightly we should walk—Candy! don't run in the road! Oh quick! Catch her!"

Mr. Colly grabbed the animal, and held her while she squirmed, and then Miss Jenns was able to go on. "We should walk straight on and turn left, and then we shall come to the farmhouse. I know the way quite well—I think. We always used to come out here when we were children."

Miss Elmfield and Mr. Colly followed her and the two troublesome dogs along the street that was lined with small houses and shops. These were left behind soon enough, and they had a long, warm walk, because the sun had come out again now that the rain was over. Away to their left was the elf's forest, still towering over the common, still puzzling scientists, news-commentators and sightseers.

They came to their turning, and went on, towards the forest now, passing a small house with a smaller garden and a dark-haired man sitting on the step reading a newspaper, a baby bawling on his thigh. There was a field with two or three shaggy horses in it next to the house, and then more fields, containing an unusual mixture of ripe and unripe, dead and live, crops. Finally, a gap in the hedge and a notice announcing, 'Farm Fresh Eggs'.

They started up the rough track to the farmhouse, a little tired now, and hot and sweaty. Miss Jenns insisted on asking the farmer's permission to view the stone, because it was only good manners. Mr. Colly thought it an unnecessary lengthening of the walk.

The owner of Devilstun Farm didn't care whether they went to see the stone or not. He didn't care whether they shut gates or not. He didn't care if they smashed down hedges. He didn't care if they rode over his crops on cart-horses. He didn't care if they set the dogs on his livestock. He didn't care about anything any more, what with his wife and daughter sick and the plants growing up around the house all the time; and his blasted farm-hand scared to leave his wife and kids in the house on their own for longer than it took him to get a drink at the 'Green Man'—not that he blamed him, mind—and all his cattle lame—and—he could go on and on. He was just unnerved. Unnerved.

They left him to keep up with his curse. Night and day he had to work to keep his house free of climbing

131

plants—or so he said. The fields they were crossing to reach the stone seemed very familiar.

"You know," said Mr. Colly, "this is the place where we lost Mrs. Surrel."

"I was thinking that," Miss Elmfield said. "We must have come another way that time, though."

When they saw the hillock in the field, and when Miss Jenns led them to the top of the hill and pointed out the slanting stone as the stone they had come to see, there was no doubt.

"The elf came here," Miss Elmfield said excitedly. "He came here for a place to hide. So that's a connection, isn't it?" She knelt down and began to grub a hole at the base of the stone. She meant to burn the salt and a crumbled pile of dirt, put the fire out with water, and bury the wet ashes.

Mr. Colly dropped the matches for her to use, and went to inspect the stone.

Miss Jenns, watching her niece pour water on to the flames of her little fire, asked, "You're *really* trying to catch a leprechaun?"

"Yes, Auntie."

"I thought you didn't believe in them! Can I stay and see him? I should love to see a leprechaun!"

"A lot of people believe in them now who didn't before, Auntie. And of course you can stay, but we're—er—going on another visit first—well, to the Devil."

Miss Jenns didn't hear her. "A real fairy!" she said. "I always wanted to see one! I *knew* that they really did exist! I knew it!"

Miss Elmfield scraped dirt over the ashes of her fire, and told her, "Auntie, I wouldn't like you to be disappointed. If you do meet the elf, you know, he won't be as you imagine. He's really very nasty. Spiteful, and he has a wicked temper."

But Miss Jenns had stars in her eyes and ears. Mr. Colly came back to see how the burning and burying had gone on. "It doesn't look as if things are going to work here, either, does it?" he asked.

Miss Elmfield, unwilling to admit defeat, got up and called for the Devil by every name she knew.

"Come out, come out, wherever you are," Mr. Colly added. He wasn't taking it seriously any more. "I think we're wasting our time now," he said. "And theirs." And then they saw Miss Jenns's face. Mouth open, eyes wide, staring and staring. They turned to see what she was staring at.

A wolf, crouched low, brindled shaggy grey fur, eyes reflecting the green dimness of the tree-shaded hill. Another wolf crept sinuously around a tree to join the first.

"Candy! Sweetie!" Miss Jenns screeched. "Come to mummy! Come to mummy quickly."

She had no need to worry about her pets. They were already racing through the beet-field, and their yapping faded into the distance.

Mr. Colly was 'hushing' and 'shushing' Miss Jenns, terrified that her noise might bring the wolves in on them. They were already creeping forward. Two thoughts kept spinning around his head; that the wolves must have come from the elf's forest; and that he had read somewhere that wolves never attack human beings. Somehow that was hard to believe now.

Mr. Colly and Miss Jenns, being further away from the centre of the hill, began to drift towards the edge, without really thinking what they were doing. The wolves split up like sheep-dogs, creeping out to them, herding them back towards the stone. When Miss Jenns made to run, the wolf did not leap for her throat, but only quickened its trot to cut her off, and turn her back. And when they were all three backed against the stone the wolves began to circle them, at too fast a speed for any of them to run past.

Mr. Colly felt the stone warm against his cheek, heard a peculiar buzzing noise and couldn't tell whether it came from the stone, from the air around, or from inside his own head. And then everything dropped away as if they were in a lift, though whether they were going up or down it was impossible to say. The buzzing became louder, seemed to be cracking their heads, and all colour became one dull grey, as all the colours of a spinning-top turn to one when it whirls.

Chapter 13

After the noise had become so loud that they couldn't hear it, only feel it; after the heat had become a heavy thing that lay on them, after the spinning had blinded them; then there was cool silence. . . . The fall stopped. The soundlessness beat on their ears like a drum. Then a whispering crept up from the quiet, grew to a rustling.

Slowly their heads cleared and they could open their eyes and see. They weren't on the hill by the stone. And of course, Miss Elmfield thought, you couldn't 'call up' so important a person as the Devil. You had to go to him.

They were standing at the end of a large room, looking down its great dusky length. The walls and the doors were covered by tapestries stitched in sprawling yellow, blue-black, brown, green-grey and white. The colours made pictures of corn, trees, grass, flowers, people, and it was from these that the whispering sound came. They were growing. They were alive.

A fire burnt in the centre of the room, a flickering of green and blue and red; and beside this fire lay long, lean dogs, thick-furred wolves, even a bear.

At the far end of the hall were two chairs—or thrones.

One was of solid black wood, patterned with gold, which caught the light and threw it back in a thousand different silvers and fire flashes. The carvings on the chair were of fruits and wheat, of animals and men and women, all alive, moving in winds that couldn't be felt. The other throne was totally black and plain. Its only decoration was the carrion crow that sat on its back.

A group of girls sat at the foot of the first, carved throne, with another tapestry spread out amongst them as they embroidered it. Part of the tapestry was pulled up over the lap of the woman who sat in the carved throne. She was a big woman, well worth looking at, with wide hips and strong arms. Her face was not pretty, but it was beautiful. Dark, slanting eyes, a nose slightly hooked, a full and smiling mouth. All around her face, and over her shoulders, down to her chair, her hair flowed, warmly red, like earth. It whisked out about her face as she shook it, before asking, "Are these the ones who've been moitherin'?"

Miss Elmfield and Mr. Colly looked at one another.

"I beg your pardon?" Miss Elmfield said.

The woman tossed her head again and her hair flared like the fire. "Ist thee that's bin rackettin'?"

"Ah!" Mr. Colly said. "Yes. I understand her. Yes. We've been trying to see the Devil, Madam, if that's what you mean. Have we arrived?"

The woman puzzled over his words as she sat on her black and gold throne. Then she said, "The Devil?"

"Would the Old One mean more to you?"

"The Old One." The woman nodded. "It's bin a long time since any o' the human kind have been wantin' to see the Old One. Why dost come now?" And the woman sat with her head tipped back, looking down her hooked nose at them.

"Well," Mr. Colly began weakly, "well, you see—Your Grace—we came to complain about a—an elf."

"An elf," said the woman, to get them to tell more. The sewing girls were glancing up at the visitors as they worked, while they pulled the long threads through. There were twelve of them, some blonde, some red-haired, like their Mistress, or ginger, some dark as November night.

Mr. Colly seemed lost for words, so Miss Elmfield explained. "He's taken four children and Mrs. Surrel."

"Is that all?" asked the woman. She stood up and the tapestry tumbled from her lap, allowing the folds of her skirt to sweep down around her feet. She was going to dismiss them. Miss Elmfield gabbled, "He lamed a farmer's cattle and made a woman and a girl sick. . . ."

"All within his rights as an elf," the woman said. Then she smiled. "I know it is bothering," she added, "since there have been no elves on Earth for so long, but there's nothing I can do about it. The elves have the right to practise their own customs, though they are different from anything else on Earth, and other living creatures are a help to them. It is within their rights to take people."

"And he's made a forest grow with wolves in it, and changed the seasons!" Miss Elmfield burst out.

There was a gasp from the sewing girls, and the woman sat down again. "Ah," she said, "that is a different thing.

F

No one is allowed to meddle with the seasons. They are mine. Time and Death belong to My Lord." She smiled at them again, and her face was more beautiful than ever. "Sit down at the fire while you are waiting. Juarn, bring them something to drink. D'Ember, will you go and find Himself, and ask him if he wishes to hear about an elf who has been changing Time and Death."

Two of the sewing girls, one tall with hair so fair that it was white, and the other shorter, plumper, with black hair, got to their feet and left the room on their separate errands.

Miss Jenns had to be pulled to the fire, she was so frightened. All the time they had been talking to the woman she had been making squeaky noises and waving her hands about so that they seemed like leaves in the winds. She didn't want to sit on the benches arranged about the fire, because of the large and untamed animals, so different from Sweetie and Candy. She wasn't quiet until one of the wolves opened one yellow eye, watching them. That eye didn't encourage the others to chatter either. The tall, fair girl came back then, and served them with large, wooden cups of pale green liquid. It tasted a lot like cider, but it was warming like whisky. It didn't take long to finish.

The red-haired woman had pulled her part of the tapestry over her knees again and was pushing a big needle, threaded with wool, through the thick cloth. "Tha must excuse me for going on with my work," she said. "But it must be finished. It is of a great importance." She bent low over her stitching, and her bright hair became just another lightish patch in the flickering

138

gloom. The whispering from the walls hissed on all around them.

Miss Elmfield sat tightly upright, one arm round her aunt, worrying about where the elf might be at this moment and what he might be doing. All this time and the Old One hadn't come, and the elf could be getting farther away, and farther away . . . and then her mind turned on her, and told her that it was impossible to be whipped away to a huge old-fashioned house where you sat down to wait for the Devil, or whatever you wanted to call him, after having talked to a woman who controlled the seasons. It was impossible, therefore she must be dreaming. She had never before had a dream where she knew that she was dreaming, but it was the only explanation. Where was the Old One? She hissed, "I hope he isn't long."

Miss Jenns whimpered again at the sound of her voice, but Mr. Colly whispered back, "I hope he is. I'm not looking forward to meeting him at all, I can tell you."

"That's a nice thing to say," she retorted, "when those children and Mrs. Surrel are with the elf."

"I can't help that," Mr. Colly said. "I still don't want to meet him."

He sat miserably on the bench, staring at the still unblinking yellow eye that watched them, and wondered and wondered what the Old One might look like. An old man with a long beard and grey clothes? A big, black, hairy sort of ape-man? He could take either of those forms. But what if he didn't look like that at all? What if he were so incredibly, hideously, staggeringly ugly that the human mind couldn't bear it and exploded? . . .

139

Perhaps he would resemble the medieval concept—those were fine, schoolteacher words, and he wished he was back in school now—and have horns, a trident, a long, spear-tipped tail, and be generally red in colour. With bat's wings. Perhaps an Egyptian touch with the body of a cart-horse, the legs of an elephant, the neck of a giraffe, and the head of a badger. Or just a shapeless mass. The mind, turned loose on the subject, could invent a thousand possibilities, ridiculous, comforting, or horrible.

He heard the swish and scratch as heavy cloth was pushed aside, and the red-haired woman say, "There thee bin, My Lord. These are the people who wished to see thee."

Now they could look up and see what the Devil was like, but they daren't. It was not a good feeling to be sitting with heaven knew what a few feet away.

At last, slowly, ready to duck his head, Mr. Colly raised his eyes. He winced once, gulped, and then whispered to Miss Elmfield, "It's all right, he's—almost —like us."

So then she looked up and saw, standing by the other throne, the carrion crow sitting on his arm, a very tall, broad-shouldered, thick-armed man. But his size wasn't the noticeable thing about him. From his head sprouted the great twelve-pointer antlers of a Royal Stag, soaring up and up, curving and gleaming. And his legs, below the knee, were hidden in harsh hair, such as grows about the legs of a stag or cart-horse, and below the hair appeared the cloven hoofs of a deer.

He was staring at them now, staring blindly, because

140

how could those eyes see? They were yellow and slanting, and the colour and pupil ran across the eye, lengthways, instead of being upright and round. They were goat's eyes. He was still staring at them, waiting for an explanation, but his eyes held theirs and they couldn't speak, couldn't break the silence until he did. A wolf, then another, and another, their shoulders heavy and shaggy with hair, loped across to lie at his feet.

The woman came to their help. "They have come to tell thee of an elf who is disturbing the seasons, My Lord. You know that the seasons belong to me, and have done since before the beginning. Thee and thy people have no business with them."

The Antlered Man turned his head, to give her the same seemingly unseeing stare. The woman went on, "The elf has altered Time as well, My Lord, and given life to that which was dead. A forest, I think it was said. These people here have come to ask that the elf be punished and the people he took be returned."

The Man turned his yellow gaze back to the three nervous members of the human kind who huddled by the fire.

"They complain of my people. Let them pray to their God."

The Man's voice came as a surprise after his long silence, after you had become sure that he couldn't speak. It was thick and deep, like mud, drawing the words out like a hound's baying, or a stag's bellow. He glared at them, waiting for their answer, but they could only stare back, voiceless. The carrion crow flapped its wings and scraped a noise way back in its throat.

"My Lord, you frighten them," said the woman, and Miss Elmfield thought that she sounded frightened too. "They come to thee, My Lord, so they must have faith in thee. And bear in mind that whatever they choose to pray to—Christ, Odin or Science—their deaths are thine."

The goat-eyed man turned back to the door-way. He said, "Dana, they are thysen. Don't run to me."

The woman left her stitching and went to his side, saying, "Call off th' elf for me, My Lord, so that he doesn't undo all my hard work."

The man with the goat's eyes smiled, and the hair stood up along the backs of the wolves, and they crept away, low to the ground; the carrion crow flew up into the rafters, screaming with terror. "Dana, My Lady, let the elf go on with his piping and I shall have many more deaths. Remember the Black Death and how many died then. It was a good time. It was a good play of mine."

The woman smiled back at him, and at her smile the rustling sound of growing things grew louder and whispered among the oaken rafter beams. "My Lord," she said, "you must help me as I help you, so that all things are equal. If you do not, all those that I favour will have everlasting life, and there will be no deaths. What will you do then, My Lord?"

The Antlered Man smiled again, and the air in the room became so icy that even the fire shuddered, and shrank into itself, and the growing tapestries were quiet for a second. "I will help thee. Then there will be life, and there will be death, balanced as before?"

"There will, My Lord," Dana said.

The Antlered Man turned to face the fire once more, and the light flashed amber in his yellow eyes, as the carrion crow fluttered to settle on his shoulder. He lowered his horned head, and stared thoughtfully at the wolves around the fire. The wolves rose and ran, one after the other, through the cloth-hung door.

The Horned Man stood motionless still, in the half-shadow, half-flame-light of the Hall, his face hidden in blackness. He flung his head up suddenly and turned his dead eyes on the red-haired woman. "The Balance," he said. "Death balanced always with life. It is tiring, Dana. I think I will not be a slave to it for very long now, only that the human kind may survive."

He began to walk about the room, light and dark, shadow and flare of light, stiff-legged as a stag. Every time he found a human figure stitched into a tapestry, he pulled out the threads that formed it, and dropped them, curling, to the floor. The three humans by the fire felt the sweat break out on them in relief when the Antlered Man ducked once more through the doorway.

"My love," Dana said to one of the sewing girls, "count how many figures My Lord has destroyed, and see that— er, let me see—that number of babies less two are sewn into this picture. Juarn, get some more drinks, wouldst, lover?"

Chapter 14

"Wheer's Mike?" Lin shrieked. "Wheer's Mike? He's gone, he is, he just went. . . ." She began to cry, high-pitched and teeth-jarring, the fingers of both hands pushed into her mouth.

The sound caused the luchorpan much pain. He hunched as if her wailing was something solid that hit him and that he wanted to duck away from. He shuddered, his face twisted. "Will yer shut that noise? Shut it! For Dana's sake will yer shut it?" Lin continued to bawl, while Mrs. Surrel fussed and tutted, and drew herself up, offended by the racket. The luchorpan brought his whistle to his mouth and blew a note that drove splinters into the ears, that shook every bone, that left the legs shaky. It easily drowned out Lin's voice, and gave her such a shock that she stopped her squalling in the middle of the highest note. The luchorpan shook his head and groaned, trying to clear his head of the blasting echo.

Five people stood on the tow-path, underneath the hawthorn tree, and looked at each other. Mrs. Surrel saw three children, two girls and a boy. Their hair stood up, they had no cardigans, no socks, no shoes, no coats.

144

Their clothes were ripped and almost as dirty as they were themselves. Tinkers' children, Mrs. Surrel thought, pulling herself up tall in her corsets, and feeling for her coat to fold it around her. But she had no coat. She looked down at her feet. No shoes, her stockings all laddered and ripped. With horrible realisation she reached her hands up to her head. No hat and her hair all over the place. There was an older boy with the three children; she saw him grin at her, laughing at her. He was the dirtiest of the lot, and dressed in the strangest clothes. His face, she thought, looked older than it ought for a boy of his size. A nasty, crafty, dirty tinker's boy. Mrs. Surrel sniffed loudly, put back her head, to show him that she was still better than he was; and then she fled along the tow-path, limping on her shoeless feet. She didn't quite know how she came to be in her present condition, and that was frightening. She thought that as soon as she got into town she would telephone her husband and ask him to fetch her. Then she could hide somewhere and wait for him.

They watched her go, and turned in again on their own circle. Lin saw her friend Shirl, grubby and untidy. Shirl saw her friend Lin, her frock torn, her shoes and socks gone, her cardigan too. They saw Chris Russel, a boy they knew because he was in the same class at school, and a man, a very little man with a tall hat, clothes with an old-fashioned cut to them, rumpled and filthy.

Lin asked, "Who're you?" because she thought she ought to know.

The little man smiled and shrugged a shoulder. "One

o' the fellars that was diggin' the canal—oh, a long time ago," he said.

The girls stared at him suspiciously. He was having them on, of course—but—there was something . . . music . . . graveyards?

"Can't be," Lin said.

The little man nodded indifferently. He put his hands into his trouser pockets, and his square coat-tails flared out over his arms.

"Oh come on," Lin said to Shirl, "I'm hungry."

They turned and hurried off together down the towpath, without looking back.

"Our mothers won't half be mad," Shirl said. "Do yer think we better try and find our shoes and things? They cost, yer know."

"We don't know where we lost 'em," Lin said. "Anyroad, I want to go home."

Shirl asked, "How long do yer reckon we've bin away?"

"I can't think. Can't be all that long but it seems like *years* to me." They reached the lock-gates and scrambled up the narrow path to the road.

Chris said to the luchorpan, "You said you'd tell me about the Russels what lived in them cottages." He could look into the elf's face almost on a level, and the more he looked, the more he remembered of some distant and foggy life.

"I did," said the elf, and smiled lopsidedly. "But I haven't the time. Not now." He pointed to the sleeping figure of a man, half-hidden in the long grass and stinkweed. "He won't sleep for long an' I've a long way to go."

146

"Where to?" Chris asked.

"The Howe. D'yer remember me tellin' yer? There's a—a girl waitin' for me there, only this high." He held his hand just below his shoulder. The girl would not have been as tall as Chris. "She must have been waitin' for—for twenty times twenty years now," the luchorpan added.

"Gaah, she'll be old, won't she?"

"She will not!" The luchorpan sounded hurt. "Am I old an' it's me she's waitin' for?"

"No," Chris said, and they stood looking at each other. The luchorpan smiled again, reached up into the hawthorn bush above his head, twisted a sprig of leaves from a branch, brought it down and twirled it in Chris's face. The leaves were brighter than they should have been, they shone like . . . not like emeralds. Emeralds would be hard and glassy alongside these leaves. The leaves shone of green mist, of sunlight under water. They sang, one of the silent tunes that the luchorpan sometimes played and that you heard with your mind, not your ears. The song filled Chris with a shivering laughter, like rippling water.

"Take 'em," said the luchorpan, and his voice was low and thick and creamy. "Take 'em an' mind yer keep 'em. Don't lose 'em, for Dana's sake, don't lose 'em. That's yer life's luck there. All together in one lump an' not scattered about where yer might miss it. D'yer hear 'em singin'? Aye—there's only you an' people like yer can hear that. Not everybody. That Lin—in a year's time she won't hear it. It'll be an impossible thing to her, an' she'll not let herself hear it. If there ever comes a time when you can't hear 'em yerself, then God keep yer is all I can say. God keep yer, 'cos we'll have no time for yer."

Chris looked up at his face, under the shadow of the hat, and the luchorpan was very serious. He looked to the leaves as they twirled between the elf's fingers, shining, singing luck.

"Go on. Take 'em," the luchorpan said.

Chris reached out, then took the leaves, spinning them on their twig. Their song filled his mind and beat with his heart. Courage and luck. He raised his head again to see the luchorpan. The elf hadn't been, up till then, the friendliest thing he'd ever met, but he said, very sadly, "Well, ta-ra then."

The luchorpan touched his hat-brim cockily with his stuck-up thumb, smiled again, and walked off in the opposite direction. Chris watched him for a little way, then walked towards the lock-gates and the town.

Toole O'Dyna saw nothing in front of him but the hall of the Howe; the hounds and the fire, his own people, Aeve, and the guests, Tobin McGraw and Michael Slater.

Thank Dana he was going back now! To some real music, and some real food. There was nothing, he thought disgustedly, that the humans could offer that could match the Howe. He paused to decide which way to go, and pointed himself in a westerly direction again. It was a long walk but he'd get there eventually. He walked through a hedge, the bushes politely stepping

148

aside to let him through. A noise from behind, a sharp, barking noise, made him turn quickly.

. Across the road from him, a bank rose steeply. Down this bank, running crouchingly through the willow-herb and nettles, long grass and bushes, came two long, shaggy shapes. He caught only a flash of them as they cut swiftly and smoothly into the grass, but he knew what they were. He knew it was no use trying to run. He sat down, just behind the hedge, and waited, whistle in hand.

The first wolf slid through the hedge, and sat grinning at him, showing its black-red throat, and its long fangs. The second wolf came through the bushes somewhere to the side and behind him, where he couldn't see it, but only feel its warm, damp breath.

He lifted his whistle and the first sighing notes of Forgetfulness lilted out. The wolf only grinned the more. Toole O'Dyna held out the pipe to the wolf, and the animal took it in its teeth and stood up, waiting for the luchorpan to follow.

Mr. Colly, Miss Elmfield and Miss Jenns were warming themselves in front of the yellow fire when the Antlered Man came back through the curtain-hung door.

This time he went straight to his black throne and sat down. Dana pushed her part of the tapestry from her lap, tossed her hair back, and smoothed her skirt. All twelve of the sewing girls scuttled over to the fire with their embroidery, out of the way. And then the curtain over the door swung inwards again, letting in the two

149

wolves and the luchorpan, who walked between them. The elf was escorted, while they watched, to the foot of the black throne, where he knelt and kept his head down. He had some idea of pleasing the Antlered Man by the kneeling, and he didn't have courage enough to look up.

The Antlered Man stared down at him until the luchorpan's shoulders began to shake. He was expecting some terrible punishment to be coming down on him every second, but time crawled on and nothing happened. At last the deathly, thick voice spoke above him.

"You are charged with the offences of disturbing the seasons in their order and disturbing also the order of Time and Death."

He said nothing else, and there was another silence while the luchorpan wondered if he was going to speak again. At last, seeing that he wasn't, the luchorpan wavered, "I did, yer Honour." He meant to speak up, but the words came out in a scratching whisper. One of the wolves grinned again, panting, its teeth dripping.

"My Lady Dana and Myself were not aware that you were awake on Earth," the Antlered Man observed, without anger, or any other feeling in his tone.

"Yer were not, yer Honour," the luchorpan whispered painfully. He added, "Me Lady." There was another, much too long, quiet.

"It has been reported to me that you raised a dead man from his grave." The carrion crow ruffled its feathers proudly and made its scraping noise.

The elf tried to speak, but his voice had dried up somewhere at the beginning of its life, in his throat. He could only nod.

150

The Antlered Man leaned forward, his elbows on the arms of his chair, his antlers overhanging the elf. He said with slow pleasure, "You knew these actions of yours have been forbidden since the beginning."

Again the elf nodded.

"You condemn yourself." He paused to let the luchorpan feel those words, then asked, "Your race still lives, luchorpan, because it swore to obey our laws. Have you obeyed?"

They waited while the elf struggled to form the words. At last he ground out, very low, "I have not, yer Honour."

The Antlered Man smiled once more, and one of the wolves growled. The Man said, "First you will return things to their correct order. Then you will be removed from life."

Dana put one finger in her mouth and bit it, and looked thoughtfully at the Horned Man beside her. The Man looked up suddenly and glared fixedly at Miss Elmfield. At first, under that evil, cold, yellow stare she couldn't think or move, but then Dana said quietly, "The names, me wench—of the people the elf took."

"Linda Windmore and Shirley Plummer, Michael Slater and Christopher Russel, and a lady called Mrs. Surrel," she gabbled out.

The Antlered Man dropped his eyes to the elf. "And the dead man that you raised."

They waited, but the elf neither spoke nor moved. The thick, hair-backed hand of the Antlered Man lifted just once, and dropped with a sharp 'tud' back on to the wooden arm of his throne. The wolves crept away

151

from him, back towards the fire, their tails between their legs. Then the luchorpan said, his voice jumpy, shaky, "Please, yer Honour, I let the lady, an' the girls, and the one boy go."

The Antlered Man leaned back and waited.

"Pl-please yer Honour, the dead man's alive, an' the boy's dead—er—removed, yer Honour."

"Removed where?" the Antlered Man asked idly, but with a deadly patience.

"Please, yer Honour, he's in the Howe. My Howe."

Another silence while they waited for what the Antlered Man would reply. A dog whined. Miss Elmfield held her breath. Then, the Man said, slow and clear, "You waste my time."

The luchorpan jumped and looked around for his whistle. The wolf which had taken it ran forward, dropped the pipe, and fled back to the safety of the hearth.

The luchorpan tipped backwards off his knees to sit down, and raised the whistle to his mouth. The tunes wouldn't come for the dryness of his mouth, but fear helped. The music was jerky, hollow, thin and rasping, but it was effective. Mike was there by the fire, as suddenly as he had vanished, looking dizzy and surprised. It was, as usual, hard for humans to believe that somebody could just appear, because to them it was impossible. But Mike stood in front of them, and that couldn't be argued with.

"Tha must go now," Dana said. "Will tha go out that way."

She pointed to another curtained door at the opposite

end of the hall, away from the thrones. With Mr. Colly leading Miss Jenns, and Miss Elmfield shepherding the still bewildered Mike, they hurried in the direction she had pointed.

Behind them the slow, cold tune of death began for Obadiah. Dana twisted away from it and covered her ears; but the Antlered Man smiled and ruffled the feathers of his terrified carrion crow.

Then they were leaning against the stone on top of the hill in the beet field. Just like that. They stepped through the door, and they were by the stone. No one spoke a word. Everyone was too relieved, astonished, but most of all—tired.

The echo of Spring, the last tune the luchorpan had played, still hummed in the air. Dana said quickly, "My Lord, tha have not allowed the elf to say a word in his own defence." She stopped, leaving the Antlered Man to see what she meant. He turned his head and stared at her with flat yellow eyes. He had no interest.

"He could tell us why he did what he did, knowing full well that it's against all the laws we made in the beginning," she said.

The Antlered Man continued to stare at her in silence. His stillness, his fixed gaze, seemed by themselves to make the room cold.

"I would like to hear his reasons, My Lord," Dana whispered.

The Antlered Man didn't look away from Dana. He said, "The Lady Dana would know why you committed

153

these crimes. Stop snivelling and tell her. Make it a good story now."

The luchorpan crumpled the hat he had taken off between his hands, and kept his eyes on the ground. He knew—everyone knew—that the Lady Dana was soft-hearted, and if he made his story good enough, maybe he'd get away scot-free. Or Irish-free. He swallowed, smiled, and said, "Me Lady, when I woke up and went out I found that the human-kind had altered the place a lot. It wasn't like it was when I was here last at all. There was papers and bottles everywhere, Me Lady, just thrown there an' left. An' all the water was dirty an' the trees cut down an' roads made hard all over the place, an' the big dirty things that go all along 'em, throwin' dust over everythin'. Please, Me Lady, it got so I couldn't stand it any more, so I played me whistle an' brought the forest back. I thought it looked better."

He took another quick glance at her, to see how she felt about it. She said, "The Earth was given to the human-kind for their use. They have made startling use of it. They've increased the length of their own lives, they've invented new animals and plants. It's not for you to say things are worse just because they look worse."

The luchorpan lowered his head. "If it please Me Lady, it's not me that sees it that way. My kind doesn't love the human-kind. The fewer of them, the happier we are, and we didn't need to make things ugly to make 'em better."

Dana smiled and said, "Aye, I know how you feel. . . . But now, tell me. Why did you alter the seasons?"

The luchorpan ducked his head again and dabbed nervously at his nose. That was more difficult to invent an excuse for: he couldn't think of a good one. He lifted his head, gave her the biggest grin he could manage, and began his story quickly, hoping not to give her enough time to think it over. "Please, Me Lady, I didn't mean it, I wasn't thinking at all, else I wouldn't have done it. I'm sorry entirely, I am. Yer see, when I saw what I'd done about the forest I thought I'll be in so much trouble from that when I'm caught I thought that it won't matter what else I've done. I thought it would be good to see Autumn in the middle of Spring. I know it's wrong now, and sure I wouldn't have done it if I'd thought, but I don't always think. I'm sorry, Me Lady, I am that, I'm sorry."

The Lady Dana smiled back at him, and his hopes rose, but then she asked smoothly, "And the man, why did you raise him and send the boy to your Howe?"

The luchorpan had hoped and hoped that she wouldn't ask him that. He saw his chances of escape fading. But still he smiled. He had a determination to win, to get out of this. He knew what he wanted for a punishment. A term of imprisonment inside the Howe. After spending four hundred years away there was no punishment he would enjoy more. He called up all his acting talents, smiled again, and said, "Please, Me Lady, that was through not thinking as well. It was. It was a long time ago when I was in the world last, an' it was gettin' to be time to go back to the Howe, an' I was goin' to travel part o' the way with a friend I had in the human-kind. Now that man I raised was the man who killed me friend in a fight, an' I used the last o' me strength in gettin' me friend to the Howe, and I went to sleep on a canal bank. So when I woke up I found the man's gran'son an' I raised the man, an' I told him how good the world was, an' I showed him all the bits of it that hadn't been changed by the human-kind, so that he thought the whole world was like that. An' then I removed his gran'son, an' brought him to life, an' then I left him to be keeping hisself in the world as it is—instead of how I'd made him think it was." He stopped, and thought over what he had said, coming to the miserable conclusion that he'd said too much. He added quickly, "I know it was wrong now, Me Lady, but I didn't think then, on me soul I didn't. I was angry, an' I only wanted me own back. I didn't think."

"It was a very cruel way of taking revenge!" Dana cried. "How could he get used to a time not his own? He'd be so frightened and lonely and helpless! I should think you've had your own back several times over by now!"

The luchorpan hung his head and looked sad and sorry. He whispered, "I'm sorry, Me Lady. I didn't think, I was angry an' I didn't think. That's the pure truth. Me Lady—when—when I'm gone, will—will yer give me love to Aeve, an' will yer say 'good-bye' to me mother for me, 'cos——" he ended on a gulp that was as genuine as an antique plastic tea-urn. Like all elves, he could tell a lie and prove it.

Dana sat back in her chair and thought, one finger in her mouth. The Antlered Man still watched her, smiling; but the luchorpan resisted the temptation to try to guess what she was thinking and kept his eyes to the floor. He thought that with bowed head and sagging shoulders he would look more broken and crushed. At last, after hours of agony, he heard Dana's voice. "My Lord, it appears to me that the elf's only crime is thoughtlessness. He made mistakes which I think anyone could have made. Don't thee think thee could let him live, on a promise of good behaviour, and perhaps some lesser punishment?"

The Antlered Man nodded. "I was waiting for thee to say that," he said.

The luchorpan clenched his fingers around his hatbrim, and silently cheered Dana on. She said, above him, "My Lord, th'art free to take the lives of anyone on Earth. Sure, thee can afford to spare the life of this one elf."

The elf could feel the Antlered Man smile. The thick, chilling voice asked, "Thee really want me to kill everyone on Earth for the sake of this one elf?"

She said, "He is here, in front of me now. So I pity him. And I can bring life to where there has been death on Earth, but he belongs to thee, and I cannot help him except through thee."

And the luchorpan told himself: 'B' th' Old One, lad, it's you that can act!'

But he hadn't won yet. The Antlered Man said, "Think, my Dana, what this elf has said: I didn't think, I didn't think. Remember that elves are untrustworthy, lying at all times sooner than tell the truth. For a thing that was not thinking he worked his revenge on the dead man well, no? Think that he dared to break the

157

rules because he thought we'd never learn of what he did. Do thee still want his life?"

"I do." And the luchorpan stopped breathing. Only the punishment to be decided now. Surely.

And right enough, the Antlered Man said, "Then I will give it thee, stubborn woman. No death without life. Luchorpan, you will go back to your Howe. My wolves will escort you there. You will stay there for the next six hundred years. You will not step outside for one minute of that time. At the end of that time you will come to Me. Luchorpan, does this please you?"

The luchorpan swallowed, with a secret and joyful hullaballoo within him, and said, "Yer Honour, I'm pleased that I still have me life."

The Antlered Man waited.

"I don't like the punishment, yer Honour. I like to be goin' about."

The Antlered Man nodded, but surely his yellow eyes saw the lie? The luchorpan's mouth twitched nervously, but then the two wolves rose, waiting for him, and he was able to go with them. He lowered his head to hide a smile.

The Antlered Man watched him go, watched the curtain fall behind him, and said, "The liar."

Chapter 15

So Linda Windmore and Shirley Plummer went home, and their parents were so delighted to see them that they shouted at them for three solid hours, slapped them for losing their clothes, and had something to nag them about for weeks to come. It was very much what the two girls had expected. Chris too. If anything else had happened they would have suspected that they'd come to the wrong houses.

They were asked many questions, by their parents, aunties, uncles, next-door-neighbours and policemen. Where had they been? was a very popular one. Lin and Shirl said that they had gone with a man, and he had taken them for a long walk around the countryside. Chris agreed with them, although he could have told them more if he'd wanted to.

What man? What did he look like? were the questions which came next. The children seemed to have difficulty in remembering. The girls finally agreed between them that he had been a little man. An unusually little man. Chris added that he wore a green hat.

Where was Michael now? Why hadn't he come home with them? Lin said that they had 'lost him'. Shirl was of the opinion that the little man had 'sent him away'. Chris pretended that he couldn't remember anything about Mike's disappearance, though he could have had a good guess at where his friend was.

Chris had tried not to show that he knew more than the girls about where they'd been, and the rest of his adventures, because he thought that he owed the luchorpan a good turn in exchange for the gift of the hawthorn leaves. And it was no good thinking that anybody could get Mike back until the luchorpan didn't want him any longer, so there was no point in telling all to the police for his sake.

Mrs. Surrel had also turned up, much to the relief of the police, but now there was one man too many. He had been found, lonely and miserable, wandering round the town. He had nowhere to go, and he knew no one in the district. His clothes were old—really old, and filthy. The policeman who first asked him what he was doing thought he was a tramp, but it soon became obvious that the man was sick. He said he'd seen his Gran'son—no, his Great Great, Great Great, Great Gran'son—killed right in front of his eyes; and that the man who had killed him had been an Irishman, a dirty little swine that couldn't be trusted no-how, a dirty, stinkin', vicious, damned, God-damned little swine.

The police were interested. They took the man to see Chris, who said that Obadiah was a friend of the Irishman. Even Chris was a bit hazy on the subject of Obadiah. But the man said 'no! He was no friend to that dirty little. . . .' He changed his mind too, suddenly said that he had no Grandson, let alone seen one killed. The police hadn't believed him anyway.

They didn't believe him when he said that he was no friend to the Irishman either. They tried to persuade him to tell them where this Irishman had gone, but he said that he didn't know. The police said that he was 'withholding information', and he soon found himself 'helping them with their inquiries'. They gave him a cell all to himself, where he could lie on the bunk, unhappy and frightened. He broke a plate, using it to slash at the veins in his wrist. It was hard work, because the fragments of platter were blunt, but he managed. He bled and bled, and wasn't left even weak. He said that he might have known, and he wouldn't try to kill himself again. He started to laugh, very long and loud, not happy laughter. Then he started to cry.

Miss Elmfield sat, exhausted, in one of the armchairs, hugging to her a warming tot of tea. Mr. Colly sprawled in the other chair. Miss Jenns had gone upstairs with her dogs and some sleeping pills, to rest.

Miss Elmfield took another sip of tea and sighed. It had been a long journey from the hill in the field. But they had got what they wanted. That was the thing to hold on to.

Mike, sitting on the settee, said, "An' I just went to this place. 'Twas the Howe, I suppose." He remembered the cave-like room, with the dirt floor, some stone to hold up the walls, some wood, parts just of hammered-

161

hard dirt and roots. There had been a fire in the centre of the room, made between stones, a fire with the same bright yellow flames as the one which their elf, Toole O'Dyna, had lit. The smoke had gone up through a hole in the roof, a hole at the end of which, very far away, was a patch of light. From above, unless looked at closely, the hole must have been like a rabbit burrow. And at one end of the room were penned some horses, like Shetlands, and some sheep, some pigs and cattle. The room stank of them.

"You say I was only there for a couple of days?" Mike said to Miss Elmfield. "It seemed like ages to me."

"It's only Thursday now," she said, "though I can hardly believe it. I lost all count of time."

"There was a lot of 'em, all little," said Mike, going back to the Howe. "Ought to have seen the kids! God knows what the babbies was like! There was the luchorpan's mate. . . ."

He remembered Tobin McGraw, who sat hunched by the fire, who didn't eat or drink. His face had been greyish-yellow, his eyes milked over. When Mike had been told the man's name, he had gone and spoken to him, but he had seldom got an answer. And the eyes of the murdered man hadn't focussed on him, but had just stared, wide and senseless, in his general direction. Mike had asked him: was he dead? And Tobin McGraw's lips had parted, and the word 'Aye' had trickled softly out, but not as if it had been spoken—more in the way of air escaping from a collapsing bellows. How was he killed? And the man raised one hand slowly to his head and pushed back the hair that covered his brow. There

162

was the cut and the hole that Obadiah had made, just the edge of it, purple and blue, puffed and bloody, disappearing into the brown hair above it.

"What did he hit yer with?" Mike had gasped.

And "Th'edge of a shovel," the dead man had replied.

And Mike had wondered why, if Toole O'Dyna thought so much of his dead human friend, he hadn't just let him be buried, instead of animating the body in this way. A ghost, like Obadiah, was much better off than this living dead man, even if a ghost never left its grave. Obadiah had said that the grave was safe and peaceful.

"Why did he send you here at all," Mike had asked, "if you was goin' to be like this?"

"He left it too late," Tobin had sighed. "He left it too late."

"There was a lot of 'em—little people, I mean," Mike said. "A lot of 'em could play things. Some had got like harps. They was better than the luchorpan, some on 'em." He paused a moment, and then added, "It was good music."

"Did they treat you well?" Miss Elmfield asked. She was half asleep.

Suddenly Mike didn't feel like talking. He said, "All right," and dived back into his mug.

There had been Aeve, very sympathetic. She had sat by him and talked to him, asked him how old he was, if he had any brothers or sisters, what did his mother look like, and was she well? And it had been Aeve who had warned him not to accept any food or drink—not if he wanted to go back home.

163

He looked at Miss Elmfield. "Can I go home now?"

She jumped, jerked awake just as she was dozing off. "Of course you can," she said, rumpling up her hair. "Would you like me to come with you?"

"No," Mike said. Turning up at home after all this time would be bad enough, without having someone there to watch. Besides, he had something to do on the way back. To make up for his rude answer he added, "I'll just go on me own. Nice tea."

"Would you like me to 'phone your parents and tell them you're coming?"

"It'd puzzle yer," Mike said. "We ain't got no 'phone. No, I'll just go, Miss, an' they'll know me when I get there."

He let himself out at the front door, ran down the path to the road and then had to stop and think. He wasn't often in this part of town, and he took a couple of wrong turnings before he found the right road to Top Church. But he stepped out then, his hand in his pocket busy with the rowan berry Aeve had given him from her necklace, and his mind busy with a tune. A tune he had heard played in the Howe, on an instrument something like a harp. He couldn't get it right. He had to translate it into the sounds a human would normally hear and the result was a sad, tired, hollow whisper of the music played in the Howe.

He hopped over the wall of Top Church—it never occurred to him to use the gate—and walked around the building, to look for Obadiah's grave. It wasn't so hard to find this time, though he had to thrash about a bit in the uncut grass, that had sprung up again after the

164

bashing he and the luchorpan had given it. He read the inscription on the stone again and laid his hand on its cold, rough surface. He had briefly met Obadiah, and he knew now, without the elf on his back, that Slater had been—well, what was called 'a good man'. A good Gran'dad. He was dead and at peace now; Mike knew that he had died for the second time when the luchorpan played the tune of death in Dana's hall, and was back in his grave. That would be a puzzle for the police, Mike thought, but he was glad that all was well with Obadiah. He wished that he could know Saranne.

It was no use wishing—not in the ordinary run of things. Wish in one hand and spit in the other, he had often been told, and see which gets full the quickest. He had made a hole in the soft dirt with his finger, made the hole bigger, dropped in the berry, and covered it up. Bury the berry, Aeve had said, on Obadiah's grave. It'll keep witches and goblins away—and elves. It'll protect your Obadiah and keep my Toole from any more trouble of that sort. He got up and walked away, through the green grass, over the wall, into the streets of Victorian houses and trees, into the streets of factories, and then into the streets of small houses. He didn't see them. His mind had fallen again into the pattern of the tune he had heard. A broken pattern.

His parents were more than pleased to see him. After the girls and Chris had come home, but not Mike, they had thought that he was gone for ever. His mother became wet-eyed, and his father silent and embarrassed; and they took him visiting around the family as if he were a new baby or husband or wife that had to be shown off. They were even saving the nagging until later.

Normally Mike would have been angry and shamed by all the fuss, preferring a bawling-out any day, but now he didn't care. Half the time he didn't hear them when they spoke to him. He was listening to something else.

He was alone a great deal after he came home. Partly of his own choice, partly because his friends found his silence boring and didn't like being ignored. His mother worried about him for a while; but she had other children to look after, and then another baby. "He'll snap out of it," she comfortably told aunties and grannies and neighbours.

She never noticed whether he did or not.